New Dimensions in

Pastoral Care

New Dimensions

in

Pastoral Care

by
WAYNE E. OATES

FORTRESS
PRESS
Philadelphia

To the Crew of

The River Assault Squadron #11

Riv. Div. III, T-111-4

The Mekong Delta, South Vietnam

Seven Combat Sailors

Contents

Preface

This brief volume began as the Zimmerman Lectures at the Lutheran Theological Seminary, Gettysburg, Pennsylvania, on May 1 and 2, 1968. I am indebted to President Donald R. Heiges and the faculty of the seminary for adding to their invitation the encouragement to publish these lectures.

I have added the last chapter on the rapprochement between pastoral care and the present social revolution. The material has been completely rewritten and is not merely a transcript of spoken lectures. I have also included an extensive bibliography of the many worthwhile studies and reports relevant to the whole field of pastoral care which I have mentioned in the text.

Lest we in pastoral care be "at ease in Zion," these pages are written to call us to new adventures into undeveloped dimensions of pastoral care.

Chapter 1

The Old and the New

in Pastoral Care

No word is more often used to describe the world we live in than *changing*. We are so accustomed to hearing of new scientific discoveries and technological breakthroughs that we may sometimes wonder if any "constants" remain at all. Part of our impression is misleading, of course; change has always been the chief ingredient of human experience and history. Only now our communications make us more aware of change, and that may be the greatest change of all. For to know about transformations around us is to be changed to a degree ourselves, not only in what we know but in how we respond.

The field of pastoral care can neither remain oblivious to change nor prevent its own change. It will either change or simply pass away, a dead thing. But if we say pastoral care *must* change, we are calling for a conscious and deliberate effort to guide the process of transformation in the field. Mere change is not necessarily growth or progress; it may be disintegration and decay. We need to be concerned about changing in a way that ministers to the new needs of persons now aware of the changing world. And we must also be dedicated to the task of building for the new by drawing on the rich treasures of the past.

1

A NEW LOOK AT OUR LEGACY

In the quest for growth in service to persons, pastors must strive to become pioneers, not faddists. There is a vital difference. The pioneer does not love new things just because they are new. He is not buffeted about by every wind of doctrine that wafts his way, striving to resolve personal anxieties by grasping at something novel. He has instead a consuming concern that endures time, a sense of direction that comes from a tutored vision if he is a young man and a persistent, unrealized dream shaped by experience if he is an older man. Pioneers always relish the lure of the yet-untried. They have deft hands that sift out the grain of true promise from the chaff of false illusion and a patient but sharp surgical skill in cutting through the red tape that stifles action. Pioneers are too few and rare to form a committee; they are not numerous enough to hold a convention; they are too busy doing what they are doing to "promote" what they are doing. They are nonchalant enough about possessions to be at home in any and all material circumstances. The real pioneers are not aliens adrift but pilgrims looking for an elusive promised land they cannot describe precisely but will recognize with rejoicing when they enter it.

In the field of pastoral care, we need pioneers who refuse to puff the pipe of peace with things as they are. They must be restless for fresh discovery. This searching is the heart of what they have learned and what they teach. The genuine pioneer does not sneer at the hard-earned gains of other pioneers, either. He stands on their shoulders to catch a better view of yet-unexplored territory.

Consequently, he who would be a pioneer has a legacy to take with him in his adventures. That legacy includes a clear definition of what pastoral care is, a definition hammered out in the experience of earlier pioneers who broke new ground to enlarge the dimensions of Christian ministry. That legacy also includes a proven methodology of teaching and learning pastoral care, known as the clinical method. These two aspects of the legacy of the pioneer need elaboration.

What Is Pastoral Care?

Pastoral care can be defined as the Christian pastor's combined fortification and confrontation of persons as persons in times of both emergency crisis and developmental crisis. Each term of this definition calls for elaboration. The *Christian pastor* is one dedicated to the care of souls in the name of a Master who came to serve and save every suffering sinner on the face of the earth. We shall have more to say of the pastor's role and the ministry of caring in chapter 2; it suffices for the present to stress the totality of the pastor's commitment to each person in his charge and to highlight his loyalty to One who lives both beyond and within his pastoral relationships. *Fortification* is the modern-day meaning of the King James word *comfort*. It means to strengthen, encourage, support, "put heart into," sustain. The appropriate biblical image is Barnabas, a "son of encouragement." *Confrontation* means to bring persons face-to-face with themselves, with one another, and with the issues of justice, mercy, and peace, integrity, truth, and understanding. *Times* means both the particular propitious moment when a person feels the need for care and the particular age level which he and his family find themselves in the process of development. *Times* means much more than *chronos,* the calendar-and-clock time of history; it means the propitious moment, the *kairos,* when eternity breaks into time and life-and-death issues are posed for the human soul. *Emergency crisis* refers to a critical moment, essentially unpredictable, which is characterized by surprise, shock, and chaos. An example of this type of crisis would be the sudden death of a young person in an accident, or perhaps an emergency requiring a critical decision about, say, open-heart surgery or a kidney transplant. A *developmental crisis* refers to a "common venture" of most people in a given culture at a given time in their lives. Examples include the birth of a baby into the home, the baptism or confirmation of a child, the marriage of persons, the departure of a first child to college, the departure of a last child from the home, retirement, and other expectable yet trying events. These have sometimes been called "developmental tasks." They are moments of achievement, celebration, separation, and reorganization of life. The pastor cares what happens at all of these times — emergency or developmental.

Inherent in this definition of pastoral care are the disciplines of pastoral care. These disciplines are the pastor's strategic and tactical avenues for expressing his care. At times of crisis, he must mobilize the strength of the Christian fellowship and bring it to bear upon people's lives. He is equipped with the Word of God and prayer to rise far enough above a given "thrown situation" to have an overview of it. Without this overview he can be no more than a tinkerer with souls. A pastor with episcopal wisdom sees to it that "drooping hands are lifted," "weak knees are strengthened," and "straight paths are made for wandering feet," so that "the lame are not put out of joint but healed," that no "root of bitterness" springs up to defile the community, and that no one sells his birthright for a single meal (Heb. 12:12–17). No pastor can live up to this high goal unless he has submitted himself to preparatory discipline long before a crisis and to renewed discipline each time he turns to strengthen others. The disciplines supply new dimensions of quality and depth to the pastor's care of the flock. Acceptance of these disciplines separates the pastorally careful from the pastorally careless. The first of the preparatory disciplines is acceptance and experience of the clinical method.

The Clinical Method

The clinical method of learning pastoral care brings the student into supervised encounters with persons in crisis in order that (1) the shepherding task might be experienced immediately and directly; (2) theory and practice might be homogenized; and (3) scientific knowledge of human relationships might be both tested by and correlated with theological insights and vice versa. At the heart of this method, then, is encounter, supervision, direct experience, a rejection of any neat distinction between the theoretical and practical, and a dialog between science and theology at the pastoral level.

These two gains of earlier pioneers are an inheritance dearly bought. We dare not loosen our grip on them. Whatever direction our own pioneering takes, these must be to us as compass and sextant are to the mariner. They are legacies that have been purchased at a high price of sacrifice and suffering. Men went hungry and taught for nothing to achieve them. Men lived through illnesses of their own. Some of them denied themselves the privilege of marriage and children. Many of them endured the sneers of fellow ministers to secure this legacy. No pioneer of today worth his salt is going to take this legacy lightly. He will not deal with it ill-advisedly or indiscreetly, but soberly, advisedly, and with gratitude to God.

There are other important features of pastoral care as received from the past that we would forget at our peril. Some of them can be traced back to the very birth of the church in Jesus' first calling of the disciples. Paul E. Johnson aptly identifies some of the basic ingredients of pastoral education in a recent article: careful selection of candidates; nurture in the fellowship of a small group; discovery and development of the individual's unique calling and gift for ministry; regular disciplines of learning; individual responsibility in relation to the needs of others; evaluation of growth through face-to-face encounters with others; the testing of beliefs in practice; and the illumination of daily work by deepened understanding and enlarged perspectives.[1] Many of these persistent characteristics have only been sharpened and expanded in the modern pastoral care movement. But there have been some decisive new emphases as well, and the would-be pioneer will benefit from a close examination of some of the more recent contributions to our heritage.

The "Life Story" Approach

One of the earliest emphases in pastoral care in the twentieth century was a recognition of the importance of the case history method. Some of the ministers who began work in the early decades encountered situations for which they were ill-prepared by their formal theological education. Their first task became one of fact-finding, of locating and defining the living realities of parishioners' experiences and thus coming to understand their problems in depth. Anton Boisen's first assignment, in 1911, was to survey churches in their economic and social setting in Missouri, Tennessee, and Kentucky. As a student Paul Johnson worked in social service institutions in New York City. Walter Rauschenbusch's *Prayers of the Social Awakening* breathes the grimy atmosphere of his pastorate in Hell's Kitchen on New York's Lower West Side. The insight and passion of the sermons of Harry Emerson Fosdick, silver-tongued orator of the pulpit, reflect his early experience with counselees struggling through trying circumstances. Reinhold Niebuhr's concern for moral man in an immoral society was born in his pastoral encounters with deprived people in Detroit.

Out of these and similar experiences there emerged an impatience with any pat answers or preconceived theological formulas for ministering to the human condition, as well as a social passion that challenged the frothy optimism of reigning theologies. To understand man was to see individual men clearly, in both their psychological and social context.

When I studied under Anton Boisen at Elgin, I learned the importance of a carefully developed "anamnesis," i.e., recorded, uninterpreted facts of what had actually happened in the life of the person to whom I ministered. This dimension of "lives in progress," history-taking, and solid appreciation of the facts of people's lives is still with us. We have refined it. We have modified our attitude about how to go about learning these "facts." However, the dimension of wanting to know the facts about persons whom we serve is woven into the pattern of contemporary pastoral care. Anton Boisen came to understand his pastoral work as the study of "living human documents." If we are faithful to the task, the skills we learn are like those of the biblical critic: Is this an original, an authentic, firsthand document? Or is it a secondary "pseudepigrapha" that makes a person's life appear to be different from the way it really was? We are painstaking in ferreting out the facts, wanting to know, as has been said, "if a thing is so; or, is it that everyone is just *saying* that it is so that other people will believe that it is so."

Psychology helped pastors to understand that a human person lives his life in stages and if we are to care for him properly we must understand him this way. The problems of one stage are not those of the next, yet each period builds upon the past and we must know the relevant information about prior stages to know the present accurately. Sociology made us aware that at each stage the social forces impinging on an individual are a vital feature of his portrait.

A Self-Emptying Attitude

A second dimension of pastoral care developed in our own time is that of a clinical methodology for expressing a concern for other people in the name of the Living God. This dimension of pastoral care has, like the importance of the life history of the individual, undergone a heavy refinement process. Charles Holman could write a book entitled *Getting Down to Cases,* but the student in the theological school would ask: "How?" John Sutherland Bonnell might tell of his own pastoral ministry, and his anecdotes were brilliant sparks from the forge of a powerful man of God at work. Yet the student himself often asked, as I did: "That fits Dr. Bonnell's role, position, experience, age, and situation in life, but how can I do this kind of thing in my role, position, experience, age, and situation in life? For me to try to do this just as he did would be like a David wearing Saul's armor. It would not fit." The student of theology may have only a shred of uniqueness. Yet with this uniqueness he must become a pastor in his own particular way. He cannot be a duplicate of any admired mentor. He must be the first of his own kind.

A method had to be found whereby the student's own uniqueness did not stand in the way but served his function as a pastor. Thus a *way* both to learn to minister to the person and to be oneself at the same time began to emerge. Rollo May, with his typical sensitive feeling for the German language, has called it *einfühlen,* "to have a sympathetic understanding of" someone or some situation. This is the kind of sympathetic understanding Jesus displayed toward the rich young man who wanted to know how to inherit eternal life. He seemed to have a "hang-up" on inheritances. Jesus looked at him — literally meaning to consider him carefully, to inspect the situation closely, to appreciate fully what is being said — and loved him. This is not a "technique" in the manipulative sense of getting at another person to push him this way or that. It is what Carl Rogers in the late forties and early fifties called an "attitudinal orientation." This orientation implied that the pastor seeks to enter into the "internal frame of reference" of the person whom he is seeking to help. He tries to create a psychological climate of understanding and warmth. Such a climate enables the parishioner to permit the pastor to enter his life-space, to come into his "personal territory of being" without being seen as an intruder, invader, or a conqueror. Rather the pastor is seen and felt to be a friend, an alter ego, a fellow collaborator facing life with the parishioner. The pastor faces life on his parishioner's behalf, not as a judge, nor as an advocate, but as a "friend of the court." Here permissiveness is seen from another point of view, that of the person in need. The permissiveness is his, not ours, to give. He permits us into his life.

On our side of the covenant, however, the self-emptying attitude can go only so far. We are still persons who have judgments — moral judgments, wisdom judgments, and judgments about our own responsibilities for others. The issue becomes, then, what to do with these?

This problem ushers in a corollary dimension of pastoral care that emerged in the late fifties and early sixties in response to the question whether we as pastors are to be passive and ethically neutral. Are we simply to be passive in the sense of being "nondirective" and only listening with no response of our own? Are we neutral in the sense that we in no way guide the person as his spiritual director? Are we to let him find his own way on the assumption that some inherent wisdom within him would guide him *if* we really entered his frame of reference and *if* we really were understanding in such a way as to communicate forgiveness and not just approval? Answers began to emerge. *Confrontation* became a fresh dimension of pastoral care with the impact of existentialist insights upon theology, philosophy, psychology, and psychiatry.

When we think of the existential emphasis, we need to do so in a more serious manner than just name-dropping an "in" word. We must go to a person such as Edmund Husserl for a clearer understanding of this problem of the pastor's "judgment," moral or pastoral, in his relationship to those whom he seeks to help, understand, and guide. Husserl said that the intersubjective world is mediated through empathy. One handles the problem of one's own value judgments not by denying their reality or validity, but by "bracketing" them for the time being as the process of empathy permits us to experience the view of reality that one's parishioner has. The pastor is suspending operations for the time being without abandoning the view of reality that has a certain signature all his own.[2]

This is essentially a phenomenological approach to pastoral ministry which calls at a minimum for a "temporary suspension of judgment." The person in crisis needs time genuinely to understand from within the way he or she sees the world. At a maximum this is a kenotic approach to pastoral care: the pastor *empties himself* of his prerogatives of judgment, his role as a representative of God, his mission to communicate the Word of God. Even though he has all these rights and privileges, he does not grasp for them or hold onto them tightly, but empties himself of them and takes upon himself the form of the person to whom he is called. This act is itself a part of the good news of the Lord Jesus Christ, whether it is called by that name or not. The reality is more important than the name.

Self-emptying as a Christian attitude is a hard-earned dimension of pastoral care. The approach has brought the ineffable gift of God's grace alive to many emerging young vicars of Christ in recent generations of theological students. Seward Hiltner and Lowell G. Colston set it forth as the central assumption of their approach to pastoral counseling in their book, *The Context of Pastoral Counseling*. They arrived at this approach as they brought pastoral care into face-to-face encounter with clinical psychology as a discipline. An interesting conclusion they reached was that when the internal judgment about a scientifically comparable set of counselees were electronically recorded and evaluated, pastoral counseling came off with a less authoritarian posture than did clinical psychology.

Pastoral Records and Research

An older dimension of pastoral care which has been securely established and must not be forsaken in behalf of some "new thing" is embedded in the last sentence of the preceding paragraph. Hiltner and Colston used the scientific method in arriving at their conclusions and developed a research design that included accurate recording of the transactions that took place between counselor and counselee, pastor and parishioner. This dimension of scientific recording and evaluation of results of pastoral work had its beginnings with the social case histories of Anton Boisen. In a brief book which received little attention because it was ahead of its time, he described his methodology of data collection and evaluation. The book was called *Problems in Religion and Life.* The title obscures the content. The author systematically describes his method of research on pastoral problems involving personal religious experience. It is a qualitative, in-depth approach, yet it appreciates the dangers of overgeneralization from a few cases and affirms the value of quantitative confirmation by statistical study.

In 1938 Richard Cabot and Russell Dicks, a medical doctor and a Protestant clergyman, respectively, collaborated on *The Art of Ministering to the Sick.* They introduced the cumulative recording of progress notes on lives in the process of change during times of crisis. Russell Dicks later perfected this method in the verbatim-recall type of pastoral record. He was awarded a certificate of merit by the National Council of Churches for this one contribution to the teaching and learning of pastoral care. The "verbatim account" is still a standard operating procedure in teaching pastoral care. We are hard-pressed to find an improvement upon it. Other pastors in times past had recorded the kinds of data that Cabot and Dicks saw and heard and experienced. But these men gave that heritage orderly shape. An old procedure was brought alive again in the scientific context in which modern pastoral care takes place.

Unfortunately, the call of Boisen, Hiltner, and Dicks for thorough record-keeping has been honored more in the breach than in the observance. It is a sad commentary upon the lack of discipline in the ministry that we do not even yet have enough regard for firsthand reports. Respect for "writing an orderly account, having followed all things closely for some time past" (Luke 1:3), is strange music to many pastors. The discipline is only occasionally accepted. Luke set down the happenings of the lives of men and women under the impact of the good news of Jesus Christ, and today we all draw spiritual nourishment from the discipline of his labors. This is a dimension of pastoral care well begun, but in need of greater nurture in the future.

If the pastor does nothing else, he can at least save and gather his pastoral letters. The Word of God in the New Testament, after all, is given largely through epistles, and letters of spiritual counsel have been a medium for the Spirit of God throughout Christian history. How grateful we are to have Luther's letters, for example, and those of countless other laborers in the cause of Christian caring.

We are being asked today whether pastoral care as a discipline, for all its protestations of having a clinical approach, has acquired a body of "hard data" that can and should be mastered by the student. The question poses a challenge that is also a landmark opportunity. Technology has provided devices that offer new vistas for recording and teaching. Supervision through closed-circuit television, video-taped interviewing, and the widespread use of cassette recorders are early indicators of untold changes in store for our discipline. Teaching machines and retrievable taped lectures can make learning easier and more effective. If we guard against the possibly dangerous side effects, such as overstandardization of teaching and the indifference that can follow total reliance on machines, the boon can be enormous.

UNEXPLORED DIMENSIONS OF PASTORAL CARE

With the angles of vision provided by the foregoing discussion of earlier dimensions of pastoral care, we are now in an advantageous position to look at what is new in the continuing development of pastoral care as a discipline. I frankly must register concern at this point as a prelude to the exploration of new territory. I fear that the first blush of success in getting established and recognized, of finding comfortable places of work, has produced a premature orthodoxy among many of us who spend our lives in the discipline. We have settled into our departments (or compartments) in the seminary curriculum, playing the games and confronting the problems of the academic establishment that the older and more sedate disciplines have contended with for years. We are all too prone to say the same things over and over again, each one pretending that what is being said is brand-new, while his peers nod and say, "Of course, the same old thing." We do not build upon one another's work as we should. This habit may guard us against the error of dashing after every new notion that comes along to tickle ours ears and tweak our fancies. We may not be faddists — but are we equipped to be pioneers? Let us look at some of the frontiers confronting us.

Pastoral Research

The first new and unexplored dimension of pastoral care is the union of service and research at the parish level. We have been quite successful in uniting service and teaching in the clinical pastoral education movement. It seems to me that this field is getting overpopulated with supervisors. There are too many chiefs and too few braves. The prestige factor involved points toward increased overpopulation with more persons ambitious to supervise others. A loss of the pioneering spirit usually is followed by everyone wanting to get on the bandwagon when a particular thing becomes an "in" procedure.

The unexplored dimension of pastoral care research is the development of descriptive research procedures, however unsophisticated, by pastors in their work in the local parish. Careful reporting of the cumulative record of dealings with one family over the whole length of one pastor's relationship to a church is needed. Georges Bernanos comes close to this in his *Diary of a Country Priest*. Refusing to see his parish as an "administrative fiction," he draws the portrait of its "face" in candid lines. Yet at no point was he derogatory, nor did he say anything that would embarrass but only those things that would elevate his people.

Seminarians would like to read carefully kept records of what actually did happen to new pastors during the first year of their parish ministry. Howard Hovde has recently written a book describing what actually happened in the care of a group of newly-wed couples as they returned to their church community. He calls it *The Neo-Married*. He accomplished this notable task while he was an active pastor of a church. Others could do the same. Even within the hospital chaplaincy, a combination of research and direct ministry to patients needs to be developed. In doing such research we must define for ourselves what research is permissible with human persons with whom our primary purpose is ministry and care. We cannot simply manipulate persons in imitation of animal experimenters, valuable as their investigations may be. Carl Levine has said it well: "We seem to forget that the human animal *is* human, that he responds not only to laboratory stimuli, but to such unquantifiable impulses as love, hatred, loneliness, and insecurity, as well as to his own peculiar concept of himself." [3] Yet we must find research and reporting techniques that further understanding while preserving the dignity of the persons in our care. I am confident it can be done.

An Empirical Study of Pastoral Home Visitation

A second unexplored dimension of pastoral care is the study of pastoral visitation in the home. Such a study should be the basis for the development of a more disciplined kind of home visitation. William C. Biers, a Catholic priest, tells me that in his opinion a unique feature of the Protestant ministry is its emphasis upon pastoral visitation. He likens it to the Catholic confessional. The clinical pastoral education movement has made much of visitation in the hospital and pastoral counseling in the church setting. By definition, pastoral counseling in its strictest meaning implies that the person comes to the pastor. They meet in the controlled setting of an office. The time factor is modulated carefully by the pastor himself. His role must be clearly defined as that of a counselor. However, knowing *how to begin this process* calls for considerable shaping and conditioning. We have usually thought of pastoral visitation in the home as a part of what Seward Hiltner called "precounseling," a means whereby the goal of counseling is set into motion.

Today, however, there is increasing need for pastoral care in the home setting. Hospital stays, for example, are getting shorter and shorter. As a result patients are busier and busier as they are dealt with more rapidly by the staff. The doctor tries to keep costs down and to make maximum use of bed space by using new medical-technological advances extensively. The new unexplored area of pastoral care is the ministry of the pastor to the patient who returns to convalesce at home. This ministering calls for pastoral visitation by letter, telephone, and in person. How is this done? I have a few offhand "rabbinical" remarks to make. But no clear study has been made. No way of closely supervising pastoral visitation has been developed.

Pastoral visitation will thrust the minister into relationships with many helping professions other then medicine. Visitation with a parolee from prison will thrust him into relationship with the parole officer. The visit to the truant school boy or girl will thrust him into relationship with the public school teacher and the truant officer. The visit to the young person who is about to drop out of school will also involve schoolteachers and principals. The visit to the indigent welfare client will put a pastor into dialog with the social worker. The visit to the young person who has won recognition in 4-H work, athletics, or scholastic achievement will put the pastor alongside the county agent, the coach, the teacher. A supportive visit to the home of persons facing a divorce can relate the pastor to the divorce court and lawyers. The visit to a young person facing the draft can relate him to local military counselors and advisers.

The pastoral visit involves planning and initiative on the part of the pastor. The pastoral visit has become so identified with the recruitment of new members for the church and the prodding of those negligent in attendance or giving that this is *the* meaning lurking in the mind of the parishioner when the pastor appears. The new dimension of pastoral care would replace this threadbare interpretation with the connotations of care, interdisciplinary healing, and genuine concern which have become so much a part of pastoral care in institutions and in counseling.

Supervised Pastoral Care in an Academic Community

A third unexplored dimension of pastoral care is the application of the tools and insights developed to the chaotic conditions on college and university campuses today. Here again one-to-one research is needed. We are weary unto death of the "my-side-your-side" rattlings over student protests, radical movements, and the like. Russell Baker in the *New York Times* of December 8, 1968, speaks of the imprisonment of college youth in permanent "kidhood," asserting that they are compelled to spend a third of their lives thinking of themselves as "kids." Kenneth Keniston has begun an important study of alienated youth in *The Uncommitted*. Probably one of the major casualties of the Vietnam war is the American educational system. As Robert Frost says, we have made a religion of education and have lived in the fond faith that knowledge will of itself take fire and light up the world. But the casual visit of a person who spends his time working with mental patients to a college campus calls for little or no shift in perspective to appreciate much of the disturbed communication and snarled-up transactions taking place around him. My point is that the campus is a relatively unexplored territory for pastoral care in our time. The disturbed identities of theological students have much of their conception and gestation on the college scene. A new dimension of pastoral care is to extend the clinical method into actual application on the college and university campus.

Pastoral Care Methodology in Other Theological Disciplines

Finally, another dimension of pastoral care yet to be developed is the extension of what has been learned through the patient application of the clinical method of education to other disciplines of the theological curriculum. In a sense it is tragic that the development of pastoral care had to follow the lines of already established, neatly defined, departmental entities. We are overcoming departmental separatism to some extent. The interdisciplinary teaching of pastoral care by the inclusion of a systematic theologian, a philosopher of religion, a professor of Christian ethics in the teaching process has been successfully tried. But it has been too much of a one-way street. What is greatly needed is the use of the empirical method in the study of such disciplines as systematic theology. For example, a research project in which I am engaged has convinced me of at least one frustrating reality. It is epitomized in a Christmas card I received from a twenty-one-year old patient, the oldest of three siblings in a family with two brothers, her mother, and her father. The card read:

> Let us trust our God
>> When the tempest assails
> For his light never dims
>> And His Love never fails
> His trust is forever
>> and will not deceive
> And he answers our call
>> when we trust and believe.

Yet this person was admitted to our hospital with the steadfast obsession that God was about to destroy her younger brother, that she could not change her clothes lest God destroy her completely, and that even though she had been a Christian since she was eleven, God was against her.

The schism between her idea about God and her emotional reactions toward God was an abyss of terror. The kind of theology we are taught and verbally espouse must in some way be brought into cauterizing contact with the way people really feel about God when they "tell it to us like it is." My contention is that systematic theology by reappraising its methods of teaching can be a new dimension of pastoral care. The older classical methods of lecture, expert-opinion expression, and "theologizing conversation" are as valid as ever. However, the use of the case method would sharpen and clarify the teaching and learning of theology as well as ethics and even biblical study.

A golden age of the teaching and learning of pastoral care was evident in Union Theological Seminary in the early 1950s. Many disciplines were involved. In the field of philosophy of religion, the late David Roberts explored the meaning of psychotherapy for a Christian view of man and went with his students to Rockland State Hospital to explore these subjects along with people of other professions. Paul Tillich explored the meaning of healing in relation to the Spirit and to salvation, a study whose fruits are evident in volume 3 of his *Systematic Theology*. John T. McNeill published his extraordinary *History of the Care of Souls.* Cyril Richardson both wrote and taught about the historical framework of the ministry to the sick. Lewis Sherrill disciplined the field of religious education with his firsthand knowledge of the psychotherapeutic process in relation to the development of personality; in deceptively simple words he wrote his profound book, *The Struggle of the Soul.*

As I began my teaching at the Southern Baptist Theological Seminary, one of my clinical supervisors, Ralph Bonacker, asked me a penetrating question: "Why do you have to start a new department? Why can you not incorporate the teaching of the care of the sick and brokenhearted into the theology department?" Of course, we went the way of all flesh. We started a new department. The American Association of Theological Schools membership as a whole has followed this compartmentalization of pastoral care into a separate discipline. One can only say, so be it.

Still, even at this late date, the dream and vision embodied in the question of my supervisor in 1944 might even now be realized. Quite by accident we stumbled across a miniature trial run of the possibilities of this new dimension of pastoral care a few years ago. We had a patient at the Louisville General Hospital who spoke only German. We asked one of our esteemed theology professors who could speak and understand German, Dr. David Mueller, to help us minister to this patient. Student, chaplain, and theology professor all collaborated in understanding and interpreting the experience of this patient. If such a transcending of the natural language barrier between German and English can be the cause of collaboration between pastoral care and other departments of the seminary curriculum, then transcending the special nomenclature of the different departments *within* the English language could be done on purpose.

Recently Dr. Harold Songer, a professor of New Testament at our seminary, spent the better part of a summer participating in and observing a program of clinical pastoral education. In the fall he established a voluntary "feedback" group in his courses in New Testament. The students were to discuss the problems of personal belief and resistance they felt in being exposed to the critical study of the New Testament. These sessions became a new adventure in learning when the resistances to learning were explored at their emotional roots and the student was met on a basis where his feelings about what he was learning were considered to be not only important but as integral to the nature of the subject matter, namely, the New Testament.

One of the persons who has begun to demonstrate a variation of this new dimension of pastoral care is Don S. Browning of the University of Chicago. He has brought the disciplines of the other portions of the curriculum into the field of pastoral care and the therapeutic understanding of human personality. In his book *Atonement and Psychotherapy,* he gives a convincing picture of what can be achieved. Liston O. Mills of Vanderbilt University has explored the relevance of the teachings of John Calvin for contemporary pastoral care, and a similar study by a Luther scholar could be made of Luther's concept of *geistliche Anfechtung.* Roland Bainton says that "there is no English equivalent" of this word. "It may be a trial sent by God to test man, or an assault by the devil to destroy man. It is all the doubt, turmoil, pang, tremor, panic, desolation, and desperation which invade the spirit of man." [4]

Yet Wilhelm Pauck's criticism of Erikson's *Young Man Luther* as being more of Erikson than Luther is a word of warning, however much truth it may have in it. The person who studies *geistliche Anfechtung* must actually be doubly competent, in both psychological know-how and Luther know-how. He cannot be a novice in either. There is a two-way demand for competency and cross-fertilization of interpretation. Too many one-way streets have been built in the theological curriculum. Much emphasis is being laid upon the idea of the elision of theological curricula in various geographical areas of the country. Interschool collaboration and the reduction of competition is a worthy goal set forth by recent studies of the American Association of Theological Schools.[5]

However, within a *single* institution, there has been a proliferation of departments because of the sensitivity to territorial invasion by the introduction of new material, concepts, and teaching methodology; the insecurity of already established professors calls for delicate introduction of collaborative rather than competitive relationships. The resistance to ecumenicity within a given institution at the point of the spiritual interpenetration of disciplines will be the last bastion of separatist anticatholicity to go. Robert Ardrey may well be right when he hypothesizes that the territorial imperative is a deeper impulse than sex, survival, or the love of power. A new dimension of pastoral care is to lead the way in relaxing the "DMZ" of departmental imperialism in the theological curriculum.

NOTES

1. Paul E. Johnson, "Fifty Years of Clinical Pastoral Education," *Journal of Pastoral Care* 22 (December 1968): 223.
2. Edmund Husserl, *Ideas: General Introduction to Pure Phenomenology,* trans. W. R. Boyce Gibson (New York: Collier Books, 1962), pp. 346, 387.
3. Carl Levine, "Communications Systems and the Mentally Ill," *ETC. A Review of General Semantics* 25:326.
4. Roland H. Bainton. *Here I Stand* (New York: Abingdon-Cokesbury, 1950), p. 42.
5. See *Theological Education,* summer 1968, supplement 2.

Chapter 2

The Minister's Self-Image and
His Capacity to Care

On July 13, 1521, Martin Luther wrote his friend Philip Melanchthon from his self-imposed exile at the Wartburg:

You extol me so much. You err tremendously in ascribing such great importance to me, as if I were so much concerned for God's case. Your high opinion of me shames me and tortures me, since — unfortunately — I sit here like a fool and hardened in leisure, pray little, do not sigh for the church of God, yet burn in a big fire of my untamed body. In short I should be ardent in spirit, but I am ardent in the flesh, in lust, in laziness, leisure, and sleepiness.[1]

THE NATURE OF THE SELF-IMAGE

As Luther looked into the mirror of his own being, he did not like what he saw. He chafed at the difference between the way others saw him and the way he saw himself. We would today say that his self-concept or self-image was "low." This quotation from Luther's letter to Melanchthon provides fellowship for many of us who feel keenly the disparity between the way others see us as ministers of the Word of God and the way we see ourselves and indicates that the present-day concern of ministers over their "image" is not a new one. It opens up the subject of the minister's self-concept or self-image and his capacity to care.

The Minister's Self-Image

If we look at the word *image* in terms of Old Testament identities and an appreciation of the commandments, we note that we are enjoined to have no graven image before the Lord our God. Too much preoccupation with this topic, therefore, would be idolatrous, putting our own image before the worship of God. This possibility of preoccupation is rarely mentioned in the psychological analysis of the problem of self-concept and self-image. Therefore, let us take it seriously for a moment at least. The central core of the anxiety over our inadequacy as a self, our weakened self-concept, is impatience that we cannot be "as God." Discussion groups of pastors and seminarians sometimes come up against cases of this kind. Occasionally there will be one or more members of the group to whom no solution short of magic removal of all difficulty or imperfection is satisfactory. Clinical procedures are discussed, tried and found wanting. Like Linus hanging onto his blanket, they cling to the feeling that they must completely solve every problem themselves or else they are total failures. They must be God or be a total zero; there is no compromise. Such all-or-nothing persons might well be reminded of the inscription over the entrance of the Hotel Dieu in Paris: *Guerir quelquefois, soulanger souvent, consoler toujours!* "To cure sometimes, to help often, to comfort always!" This motto recognizes the properly focused responsibility of a caring pastor without inflating his self-concept to the point of "playing God."

If we search for understanding of the self-concept or self-image, we are helped by examining the Greek word *eikōn,* as it is used in Matt. 22:20, when the Pharisees tested Jesus by asking him to tell them whether it was lawful to pay taxes to Caesar. Jesus, being conscious of their ill intentions, asked for and received a Roman coin. He said to them,

"Whose *eikōn* and inscription is this?" It was the image of
Caesar. They were to render unto him their taxes, but they
were not to elevate him to the place of God. Paul Tillich
defined the "Protestant principle" as the protest against
putting anything or anyone in the place of God, of absolu-
tizing the relative and thus opening our lives to demonic
possession. Carl Jung spoke of a complex as one of the part-
processes of life exercising dominion over the whole. Plato
said that sin is the rising up of a part of the soul against
the whole. But to put these insights into effect as a pastor
is to be iconoclastic. It means to be loyal to God above all
— not to self, not to a selected few, not to any institution
or position. It means to refuse to become merely the private
chaplain of three or four privileged families in the church
to the neglect of the total community. These families may
need a chaplain, but not by means of a "quick-claim deed"
that subtly excludes other people. Also, the iconoclastic
pastor refuses to become a "single-issue" preacher with only
one cause as *the* ultimate in pastoral ministry. Single issues
such as alcohol control, labor-management reconciliation,
racial justice, and antiwar causes all require pastoral attention. Yet, no one issue can capture a minister for its "vest
pocket" any more than can a powerful family "buy" a pastor. The iconoclast challenges the hearthstone gods who
would make of the Christian faith a reenforcer of the demands of a patriarchal or matriarchal family situation. To
encourage young persons to leave father and mother and
follow after the Lord Jesus Christ, to cleave to husband or
wife and establish a set of directions of their own, is the
task of a pastor. At the same time, it is to sustain the same
mothers and fathers and to call them out of idolatry of
their children now grown. To call for this casting down
of every high thing that exalts itself against the knowledge
of God requires of the pastor that he even be stern at later

stages of grief when the bereaved are tempted to worship
the dead. Yet the iconoclastic responsibility of the pastor
is not merely negative; it consists of far more than getting
into the safety of the pulpit and attacking when people
cannot answer back. It is rather a principle designed to lead
men to no one but the Lord. The responsibility often comes
as it did with Jeremiah, when he spoke to King Zedekiah
late at night in response to the request: "Is there any word
from the Lord?" (Jer. 37:17).

Ministers Breaking Down?

The minister's self-image is too often made up of certain
idols of the marketplace, consisting of the minister's concept
of what he *thinks* his people expect of him. Some years ago
an article appeared in one of the popular magazines saying
that more and more ministers were breaking down because
of overwork in meeting the trivial, housekeeping, administrative chores of the congregations. Research gave some
comfort to this point of view in that one survey showed that
two-fifths of the minister's time was spent in administrative
tasks. However, the same survey reported that these actions
were prompted by what the pastor *thought* that people
expected of him. But when Charles Y. Glock and Philip
Roos studied twelve Lutheran congregations they discovered
that the congregations actually expected and approved
activities quite different from the ones ministers perceived
as their expectations. They found that congregations appreciated pastoral calling on members and nonmembers most
and attending church meetings and office trivia least.[2]

Are Ministers Leaving the Ministry?

As we moved through the sixties, another popular impression affected the minister's self-image. Many articles

emphasized the way more and more ministers were leaving the ministry. Instead of breaking down, ministers are "breaking out" of the ministry. A part of this trend is said to root in the domestic concerns of pastors: they do not want their economic security to be jeopardized each time they disagree with a church leader. They do not want their families to be subjected to either emotional or economic insecurity because they exercise their prophetic ministry. A part of this problem is the lack of economic support of the ministry. One study of dropouts from the ministry found that many of them were "cash-outs" more than they were "dropouts."

A part of the leaving of the ministry has been the feeling of some men that the institution of the parish church itself is passé and that secular forms of ministry such as the poverty program, the Peace Corps, the lay witnesses who are employed at a secular task are much more relevant. In other words, a lay-service conception of ministry has become prevalent. I regularly meet students of various denominations who can see no earthly reason at all for being ordained. To them it is merely a procedure for pleasing the establishment of the denomination or the civil government.

A Pastoral Breakthrough

In the most recent struggles among and within ministers concerning their own image or concept of themselves as ministers, a new voice is being heard faintly. I hope that it is heard more clearly. This voice brings a newer and braver message about the minister's conception of himself in the world of his work. James Dittes of Yale University Divinity School in his book *The Church in the Way* has expressed the new voice. He says that we as ministers have been bemoaning ourselves because the church as an institution is in the way of the goals *we* want to achieve. The church resists by apathy, criticism of our character, charges against

our interest in money, and refusal to come to our meetings.
Dittes says that similar resistances appear in the relationship
between the individual counselor and counselee, the psycho-
therapist and the patient. The psychiatric patient is non-
communicative and apathetic to the doctor's attempts to
heal him; he tells him that he does not know whether he
wants him to heal him or not; he complains that the doctor
only wants his money; he is late to appointments, breaks
them, or refuses to make another; he says that the doctor
has suggested that he do many evil and wrong things; and
finally he quits the doctor and begins to look for help elsewhere.

Yet a good doctor takes these resistances as challenges to
his skill as a physician; he does not introject them into his
own self-image and thereby invalidate his calling as a doctor. Yet this is precisely what the minister does. He takes
resistances he meets as causes for uncertainty, disillusion-
ment, and resignation. Or he reacts internally and lets the
whole thing somatize into an illness. Or he begins to act
out his own reactions to personal rejection by becoming a
delinquent in terms of incompetence and passive-aggressive
laziness or in terms of some immoral "Peck's bad boy" reaction.

Dittes documents ways in which difficult administrative
problems in and of themselves present a challenge to the
stature of the pastor as a caring person. He is not alone in
the point of view he has taken. The earlier work of K. R.
Andrews, *The Case Method of Teaching Human Relations
and Administration,* sets forth a similar point of view,
although it was not as vividly stated. We are living in an
age of administration. The current challenge and hope for
a breakthrough — not a breakdown or a breakout — in the
ministry is for the minister to learn to see himself as one
who cares for, heals, and brings to maturity the structures

of the church with courage and confidence. It may mean that we shall return to a pattern of earning our living with our own hands so that our voice might be free. If so, then we will not be the first pastors who have done this. Paul, Aquila, and Priscilla worked as tentmakers during the week, and Paul preached on the sabbath, persuading both Jews and Greeks concerning the way of Christ (Acts 18:1–4).

But the matter of our self-concept is much deeper than our economic security. Our integrity as persons made in the image of God and as persons for whom Christ died is no different from the integrity of those who resist us, for they too are similarly persons made in the image of God and for whom Christ died. The real issue of our self-respect rests on our confusion of being "nice" and "sweet" with people, with being genuine, honest, and open in relation to them. Humility is best understood as a combination of honesty, genuineness, and teachability. Psychotherapists call this "ego strength," "human strength," "personal integrity," and the like. Regardless of what our particular occupation may be, we can be so bent on being nice that we are willing to say and promise anything to keep people's momentary good-will. But then we will have lost our integrity. Or we may reveal the same lack of integrity by being bent on offending everyone about everything. Both turn us into salt that has lost its savor and make us fit for nothing.

We need, then, a breakthrough in our conception of ourselves as ministers that will not block our function and cause us to stumble over the business of images for too long. If we look in our own English language, we will see that as a noun this word *image* means something that possesses or displays the qualities of a reality to such a degree as to bring that reality vividly to mind. The minister in this sense is a person who has certain qualities that are vivid in the minds of persons when the word *minister* is mentioned. I could hope that some of these vivid qualities would be: first, the minister cares enough for his people to defend them from exploitation; second, he trusts them enough to care for them in ways that may or may not cause them to like him; and third, he has basic skills and knowledge that enable him to function by principle and not by magic or superstition. As a verb the word *image* (and it *can* be used as a verb) means "to represent." We represent the Lord Jesus Christ; we represent hope in a lively and graphic manner; we represent both the goodness and the severity of God.

In all this study thus far, we are consistently warned of the possibility of idolatry and playing God. We are commanded to be willing to break down any false image that erects itself against the knowledge of God. We are prompted to think of ourselves as being representative of God, Christ, and the Holy Spirit. This thought, rightly perceived and genuinely felt, produces a confident humility, the fertile seed of good sense and courage.

THE MAKING OF THE MINISTER'S IMAGE

Coming to Grips with Our Heritage

By training I am a teacher, by calling I am a minister of the Christian faith, by trade I am a weaver. I have a heritage of having come from the weaving shops of the cotton mills of North and South Carolina. I learned as a weaver that when anything went wrong in the cloth I was weaving the first thing to do was to look into the pattern from which the cloth was being woven. Let me use this simple illustration as a symbol of the making of the image of the minister as he sees himself. The behavior and thinking of a minister are woven according to the pattern of his conception of himself. They are vividly and graphically shaped by that pattern of life, the self-image. One way for you to get at this image for yourself would be for you to take a blank sheet of paper and write at the top of the page the following words: "*I am the kind of person that. . . .*" Then list the first ten things that come into your mind as to what you think when you declare: "I am the kind of person that. . . ." You hear people making such statements all the time. "I am the kind of person that if a person calls me a liar, I will never have anything else to do with him." "I am the kind of person that when I get into a room where there is a serious discussion going on, I let everybody else in the room express their opinions before I express mine." "I am the kind of person that never opens up to people because I am afraid of getting hurt."

When you finish your list of things that you would use to finish this sentence, you will have something of a tracing of the image of yourself that has been *woven* into your being through the years of your personal history. Also, you will find the kinds of images that have been *stamped* onto your consciousness by your education. We have learned to print designs on materials so effectively that you must handle the cloth and look at both sides of it before you can tell whether the pattern was woven in or stamped on. They are even making flowers now; we must feel and smell them to see whether they are living flowers or artificial!

Herein lies much of the confusion we experience in our efforts to actualize our care of other persons. We have been taught that we *should* be and we carry these ideas as a "printed-on" set of intellectualisms. However, when we get into the grimy rice paddies of the muddy terrain known as the pastorate, we tend to survive or not survive on the conditions of our "woven-in" response to life, most of which we cannot even put into words to ourselves, much less to others. We rarely function effectively in terms of our printed-on concepts. Sigmund Freud's experience of having been pushed around by Christians was woven into his thinking, feeling, and writing. This experience, more than his medical education, influenced his attitude toward religion. A person brought up in a ghetto may be sensitive. His sensitivity is his strength in times when sensitivity is needed. Yet his sensitivity is his Achilles' heel when he needs the serenity to recognize and accept the things that can only be changed slowly.

The crucial challenge of the gospel of Jesus Christ is how through participation in Christ we can turn the curse character of our past into tools of ministry for the present. The child of a poor home who had to invent his own games, make his own toys, find his own books to read, borrow a book rather than buy it, walk rather than ride, may look on all these things as blots on his escutcheon because of poverty. But in the fullness of time as a minister he becomes the kind of independent person who cannot use other people's sermons, he must make his own; he cannot function very well with a textbook that is assigned and which he must read, he must find journal articles that are more recent; he learns his sermon illustrations from watching people as he takes long walks, even though the church may furnish him with a car and money to buy books of illustrations. That which may seem to be meant to him for evil, God meant to him for good. He cannot react with the enchantment of ministers from privileged families, as if the new thing about the inner city and poverty were a *discovery*. He reacts to it as a memory recovered.

By way of transition, then, we can say that sometimes our own woven-in heritage and our more recent education may collide to stalemate our function as helping persons. But we can clarify this confusion by coming to grips with our own heritage. That heritage *can* be a resource, a strength, a source of uniqueness in our caring for people. That heritage need not be a hindrance, a blockage, or a continuing source

of conflict between what few things we have been able to
learn in our education and the many, many things we were
before.

"Propriate Strivings" and the Minister's Self-Image

In the making of a self-image as a caring person, each of
us needs to underline the importance of what Gordon
Allport has called our "propriate strivings." They are the
second source of our self-image. Allport says that the center
of a person's being — quite in addition to, over and above,
and even in spite of his personal heritage — is a person's own
individual resolves, driving intentions, and personal commitments in his own life. You can recall the personal resolves
you have made. They include the promises that we made to
someone else and commitments we made to ourselves. Let
me challenge you to write out another sheet. On this sheet
say: *"God being my helper, I have decided in years past
that. . . ."* Now put ten or twelve things one right after another. If you have made this list, you have something that
stands more at the center of your self-image than the other
list that you made. For example, you might have stopped in
the middle of a very menial job at which you were employed
and said, "There must be some better way to make a living,
and, God being my helper, I am going to find it." Or you
may have become completely bored with a field of study
and said, "God being my helper, I am going to find something that is less repetitious and boring than this." You
may have defied all the efforts of your kinsmen and friends to
deter you from the privacy of your love of books and made
a break with your whole culture and turned to become a
teacher. Allport tells the story of Amundsen, whose teenage
friends thought he was crazy when he steeped himself in
knowledge about the Antarctic and vowed that he would
someday go there. But it was in the Antarctic, after several

successful discoveries, that Amundsen later died trying to rescue a less experienced explorer.

You as a pastor, having taken your first, second, or third pastoral charge, may have come to a Rubicon in your life. You may have made a resolve as to what you will not do to maintain another person's friendship, even though you are a minister. You will make tents, return to the trade of your youth, or cast yourself upon the sheer grace of God before you will be a part of preying upon the sympathies of widows and neglecting the needs of orphans to accomplish some ecclesiastical or professional ambition. When you make such a resolve, it becomes a part of your integrity, which is another name for your self-image. Underneath all these resolves is a reciprocity between setting goals for yourself and setting limits for yourself and for those persons about you. As Martin Buber says:

A very important problem in my thinking is the problem of limits. Meaning, I do something, I try something, I will something, and I give all my thoughts in existence into this doing. And then I come at a certain moment to a wall, to a boundary, to a limit that I cannot, *I cannot* ignore.

Buber goes on to say that in his effort to establish a caring dialog for other persons he slams into these same limits of dialog:

. . . even in dialogue, full dialogue, there is a limit set. . . . I can talk to a schizophrenic person as far as he is willing to let me into his particular world that is his own, and that in general he does not want to have you come in, or other people. But he lets some people in. And so he may let me in, too, but in the moment that he shuts himself, I cannot go on. And the same, only in a terrible, terrifyingly strong manner is the paranoid. He does not open himself and he does not shut himself. He *is* shut.[3]

In other words, Buber is saying that real mutuality is one of the possibilities of human dialog. The absence of mutuality is one of the stark facts or necessities of human life. Erikson reenforces this idea by saying that mutuality is the generator of hope.[4]

Out of this involved discussion comes a snowcapped mountain of truth in the distance as to what a pastor really is when he "images" himself aright. *He is a harbinger of hope.* What hope is there when seemingly all mutuality in a relationship of care is gone? The person *is* shut to you. You can only stand and wait. Yet the pastor is one who never gives up the hope of dialog. He remains faithful to the possibility of communication and keeps open to it. This is his resolve, his commitment. He does not judge himself as a success or a failure on the basis of whether those for whom he cares open up to him. He judges himself in terms of his own fidelity to the person, open or closed. Was he faithful? The witness of the Great Judge is not success. He did not say, "Well done, thou good and successful servant. He did say, "Well done, thou good and *faithful* servant."

Emotional Reciprocity and the Minister's Self-Image

A third source of our self-image comes from those to whom we have opened ourselves and with whom we have experienced basic trust and genuine dialog filled with mutuality. If there is weakness in our self-image, the malnutrition probably is at this point. Usually these persons have been our own teachers and peers with whom we have participated in expanding experiences and shared learning. With these persons we are identified, not as children deifying an authority figure but as models with whom we have cast our lot in the struggle for survival, in the development of our own psychic space. In its sophomoric state, this kind of fresh, green growth in our self-image and our capacity to care can be somewhat amusing. James Reston has been for years the epitome of all that the *New York Times* stands for. Gay Talese describes him in *The Kingdom and the Power*:

To the younger men on the staff, it was *Reston* who personified whatever grandeur The Times had, not the high priests in New York, and when one of his reporters was offered a much better job on another paper, he was very slow in accepting it. It meant leaving Scotty [Reston's nickname]. Some reporters were so inspired by Reston's manner and talent that they tried to imitate him, one going so far as to dress like him, switching to bow ties and buttondown shirts, to smoke a pipe like him, to walk with his bounce and glitter, to try to mimic the way he spoke. . . .[5]

This adulation is borrowed selfhood, a forged affidavit of a self-image. Yet out of it can come the beginnings of a rude awakening in a person that such style in another person must indeed point to a possible uniqueness that one has himself. Your teachers and mine have woven their identity into our self-image. But they have served us best when they refused to settle for a copy of themselves and believed in our own uniqueness when we betrayed our own disbelief in ourselves by merely copying them. Their very believing in us brought into being the bold relief of the fingerprints of our own individuality. They pushed us until *we* settled for nothing less than that which we ourselves uniquely had to offer in caring for others. They may have pushed us so hard that for a time or for all time we were alienated from them and angered by them. But like them or not, they made us inescapably *ourselves* before God, not themselves. This experience was more than our own recognition of our adolescent imitating. It was painful parturition. Then we could turn and care for others because we had learned to be ourselves, the self that God gave us and for whom Christ died.

Community Expectations and the Minister's Self-Image

Finally, we come back to the expectations of our community, those which they have conferred upon by reason of the confidence they have in us that we can be a vivid and genuine representation of the eternal God in Jesus Christ. The crucial question in coming to full stature in our self-image is whether or not we are willing to take upon ourselves *any* adult role in life or not; the ministry is just one of many mature roles. Some may cling to the fantasy that they can be perpetual adolescents. Yet we know we cannot will everything and in reality cannot become *any*thing. Running from one role to another, we may act as if life were a permanent masquerade party. We appear this way now, that way then, and *any other* way we choose *any* time later. But once Scotty Reston's reporters decided to be reporters in their own right, they ceased to depend on the bow ties, the buttondown collar, the eccentric walk for a self-image. They had confidence in their own being and appearance. We, as pastors, put on the whole armor of God *as pastor.* We realize that this is for real. We really are where the good news needs to be told as it is. Then we meet people all around who need to know that somebody cares whether they live or die, who has time to take them seriously and will follow through and never forsake them. Then we have done with lesser things and being able to care becomes the chief satisfaction of living to us. We are not living on the borrowed capital of other men's selfhood. We have become self-giving spirits in our own right.

THE REPLENISHMENT OF THE MINISTER'S SELF-IMAGE

We ministers do more than our share of *rumination* and mistake it for prayer. This word is taken originally from animal husbandry and refers to a cow chewing its cud. In a cow the cud is that portion of food brought up from the stomach a second time for rechewing. Medically speaking, this physical act of rechewing points to one meaning of the word for human beings. It means that a person has not properly or completely chewed something and therefore regurgitates what is undigested. We use this word in the field of psychology and psychiatry to refer to thought processes that recur again and again in a cycle that cannot be stopped. We turn experiences of the past over and over again in our minds. Regardless of how much we think about the unmanageable thought, it will not come right. It is one of the characteristics of two particular forms of pastoral acedia which beset ministers' lives.

Acedia in the Middle Ages was thought of as one of the seven deadly sins, a sort of spiritual torpor, apathy, and ennui. The spirit "sours," as it were. The two forms of it today which beset ministers and produce a ruminative pattern of thought are *scrupulosity* and *undigested intellectual ideas* at the "gut level" of emotional assimilation. The end result of this state in ministers' concepts of themselves is one of emotional depletion, debility, feelings of fatigue, worry, and inadequacy, lack of zest and interest, draining of enthusiasm. Often it is accompanied by a persistent depression and somatic symptoms of physical indigestion and headaches.

I have chosen to call this condition the depletion of the self-image and to suggest that this ruminative way of life can become chronic if specific measures to replenish the self-image of the person are not taken. It is one thing to curse the darkness of depletion and it is another to take carefully tested clinical procedures for the replenishment of the self-image of the minister himself.

The Search for the Cause

The minister in a state of emotional depletion begins to do what anyone else does: look for a "cause" or set of "causes" to "blame" for his trouble. It is simply not so that the minister always and in every case projects the blame for his plight on others. At least as often he is likely to find a batch of personal faults in himself. One of the faults most commonly used by ministers is to look at their education and blame the lack of this, that, or the other kind of training. It is tangible. It is specific. It is something a minister can get his hands on and bite into, as it were. From where I sit as a professor in a theological school, I read many letters from ministers who are looking for more education. However, I discover that as often as not they are really looking for one of the deeper sources of replenishing their self-image: fellowship with someone who cares what happens to them, a group of like-minded persons with whom they can have personal fellowship, with whom they can be "just as they are" without explanation. When the right conditions appear, much that psychotherapists have previously considered as "unconscious" to these ministers is material they have been acutely aware of but up to this time have considered none of the business of other people. They have cherished their feelings in a desperate attempt to have their own private lives. Yet the price of it has been a deep loneliness. Therefore, their latching on to educational adventures is sincere and real. They do need "retooling" for new demands. But at the base of the need lies a deeper one: fellowship and genuine acceptance of the persons they really are and know themselves to be.

A way of continually replenishing the self-image, therefore, would be the group practice of the ministry. Ministers now in action could become closer colleagues and meet as a group regularly for two purposes: correlating their efforts as disciplined and professionally equipped ministers, and participating in each other's inner concerns. Some ministries can best be practiced on a group basis: premarital guidance

and counseling, the constant attention to families with critical illnesses, the ministry to families who are related to
more than one congregation (as in the interfaith and interdenominational marriage), and the joint "covering for each
other" when denominational and professional meetings pull
men out of the parish. Similarly, pastors in such a group
could "take each other's calls" when they were out of town
for a brief two-day vacation after having worked day and
night for long periods.

Being a Husband

The replenishment of the minister's self-image can also
happen through an agonizing reappraisal of his conception
of himself as a husband and his response to his wife as his
wife. A rather monotonous clinical picture appears in settings where I work with doctors in the treatment of ministers: the minister and his wife are *out of reach* of what each
has to give to the other. They may have married for a variety
of reasons not dissimilar to what prompts other professional
persons, such as doctors, lawyers, politicians, and entertain-
ers to marry each other. These reasons may be that they are
both interested in and involved in the same profession, that
they can help each other through school, or that they see
each other as trophies, i.e., the minister sees the wife-to-be
as a trophy because she is a good musician, because she is
educated in the know-how of his denomination, or because
she is enthusiastic about the same particular cause, theological perspective, or kind of reading he likes.

Yet, in the grimy task of the day-to-day operation of the
home and church, these particular reasons are like glue that
has been oversold for its power to hold things together. The
real need each has is for emotional first aid from the other
after the battles of spiritual combat outside the home. They
need access to the other's support, trust, and reassurance.

This relationship is one of the main sources of the constant replenishment of the self-image. Without it, over a period of years a minister and his wife begin to see themselves as individual "zeros," tasteless and bored with each other. The sexual dimensions of this condition are important but not paramount. The paramount need is basic trust, the ability to peel off the social role of being a minister when one closes the door of his own home behind him, and the ability to sense that his wife *needs* him to do just that too, and also to appreciate her for her own sake and her own sake alone. Thus they have access to the sustaining power of each other as persons that transcends any functions they may fulfill in the church or in any other outside social setting. The minister needs to be appreciated, loved, and trusted for his own sake and not *because* or by reason of his being a minister. His wife, in turn, needs to be appreciated for her own sake and not objectified as a "minister's helpmate." She can become the latter only if the trust precedes it. He needs to be cared for by her *as her husband* and not as her pastor. She needs to be cared for by her husband *as his wife,* not as his parishioner.

We as ministers are drained of energy in the constant, twenty-four-hour-a-day defense of ideals and institutions to which we have committed ourselves. One minister's wife said, "My husband runs himself to death to keep up with the goals he has set for the congregation." Yet she and he shared this appraisal, not as her criticism of him but as a "shared appraisal" which she and he realized together. He gave her the "speaker's role" for a change. They enjoyed it in a rollicking sense of humor that was for a time a bit of private humor all their own. Only because of a most lasting and profound friendship was I permitted a glimpse of these two persons replenishing each other's sense of personal worth.

Any man or woman needs such replenishment and support. Neither demands that the other always agree with him or her or even be *consistent*. As Douglas Steere said recently, "I am not always persuaded of my own opinions." Yet to admit this kind of contradiction within oneself to one's mate means letting down our guards and opening up. John Steinbeck's Susy in *Sweet Thursday* says: "I want a guy that is wide open. I want him to be a real guy, maybe even a tough guy, but I want a window in him. He can have his dukes up every other place but not with me. And he's got to need the hell out of me. He's got to be the kind of guy that if he ain't got me he ain't got nothing. And brother, that guy's going to have something."[6]

Being a Father

A third source of emotional replenishment for the minister's self-image is available in his children. Yet this source becomes a drag and a drain if the minister sees his children as reflectors of his prestige as a minister. If, instead, he can permit them to be themselves, hear their aspirations without drowning them out with his own preset goals for them, then the younger persons can contribute *to him* of themselves. He need not be the all-wise, all-powerful, and all-sufficient one. As his sons and daughters grow older, he can increasingly establish "adult-to-adult" conversations with them about stresses and problems in his own job. He can profit by asking for their serious appraisal of important issues. They can be edifying and in turn become informed if the minister has the teachableness to confer with them.

What otherwise can be just one more "administrative headache," namely, "making rules" for the "kids," can be vastly enriching in the joint enterprise of mutual decision-making. What are the laws of decision-making? The law of available data requires data collection about any decision.

The law of the available time in which to make a decision separates emergency decisions from those that can wait awhile. The law of prior commitments sets certain limits on the kinds of new covenants one can make. Could not these guidelines become bases of arriving at common decisions rather than the use of arbitrary "rule-making" where one person not only carries all the power but also all the loneliness in a family?

Gradually the minister's image of himself is replenished as he intimately collaborates with his sons and daughters in the fine art of decision-making. Likewise, they develop the ability to converse with him as a senior colleague rather than as a game warden for them as a bunch of kids. If decisions are made and prove to be unwise they can be rethought and revamped. If they are proven by the tests of time, experimentation, and reappraisal, then they become sources of satisfaction for both pastor and the sons and daughters.

Breaking the Routine

Still a fourth source of replenishment of the self-image of the minister is needed by him and his family. They need to break the routine often. The day off each week and the month's vacation each year do not come into reality nearly enough. However, the minister who has other people to take emergency calls in a group ministry may often take one day or two days and "drop out of sight" either alone or with his family. This need suggests that the minister has not appraised the importance of the commandment to keep the sabbath. He himself *works* on the sabbath. Many times his work requires that he work two shifts, night and day, for several days in a row. When this happens, he should accrue days and make up for them with rest, retreat, and renewal.

If our Lord Jesus Christ — in his short earthly ministry — departed from the multitude without shame or explanation, can we not also be wise as serpents and harmless as doves in doing so ourselves? His competence was replenished regularly by getting *away from people*.

The Eternal God does not wring his hands with anxiety when we break the routine, do not show up at all the meetings, and fail to prove to ourselves and others that we are indispensable by our much-doing. He as the Creator who made us in his own image and for whom he sent his Son in lavish love, however, does have his own image violated by our low self-valuation. He would replenish our self-image by reminding us that he is our Creator and Redeemer:

> Why do you say, O Jacob,
>   and speak, O Israel,
> "My way is hid from the Lord,
>   and my right is disregarded by my God"?
> Have you not known? Have you not heard?
> The Lord is the everlasting God,
>   the Creator of the ends of the earth.
> He does not faint or grow weary,
>   his understanding is unsearchable.
> He gives power to the faint,
>   and to him who has no might he increases strength.
> Even youths shall faint and be weary,
>   and young men shall fall exhausted;
> but they who wait for the lord shall renew their strength,
>   they shall mount up with wings like eagles,
> they shall run and not be weary,
>   they shall walk and not faint.
>
>   (Isa. 40:27–31.)

The Stewardship of Solitude

The minister's self-image at its heart, however, is replenished or impoverished by his attitude toward his solitariness, by his stewardship of his solitude. Here he is either devout or he is not. Ralph McGill, in a column on an interview with Carl Sandburg, caught something akin to the idea of the stewardship of loneliness from Sandburg. He quoted Sandburg as saying:

"You know . . . one of the big jobs a person has to learn is how to live with loneliness. Too many persons allow loneliness to take them over. It is necessary to have within oneself the ability to use loneliness. Time is the coin of your life. You spend it. Do not allow others to spend it for you. . . ."[7]

The "nerve" required to decide how to spend your time yourself is a near-orneriness in a pastor that lets people know that he is an inner-directed man, unswayed by their whims. Yet they also have a subtle awareness that here is a person who is intimately in touch with the Lord, who enables him to know, as Jesus is described by the Johannine evangelist as knowing, that ". . . he had come from God and was going to God . . ." (John 13:3). This knowledge is the internal replenishment by God of any man's self-image, especially a minister's.

NOTES

1. Krodel, *Letters, Luther's Works* 48:257.
2. Charles Y. Glock and Philip Roos, "Parishioners' View of How Ministers Spend Their Time," *Review of Religious Research,* spring 1961, pp. 170-75.
3. Martin Buber, *The Knowledge of Man: Selected Essays,* ed. Maurice Friedman (New York: Harper and Row, Torchbooks, 1966), p. 175.
4. Erikson, *Insight and Responsibility,* pp. 231 ff.
5. Gay Talese, *The Kingdom and the Power* (Cleveland, Ohio: World, 1969). Quoted from an excerpt in *Harper's Magazine,* January 1969, p. 61.
6. John Steinbeck, *Sweet Thursday* (New York: Bantam Books, 1961), p. 165.
7. *Louisville Times,* January 18, 1966.

Chapter 3

The Minister as a
Professing Professional

There are signs that the contemporary minister is beginning to catch on that his real job is to be a provocateur who
stimulates the right questions rather than to be a repository
of all the answers. He is a heuristic teacher and clinician.
He prompts the people of God to become a posse of hunters
rather than a nest of solution-givers. As an individual counselor he stimulates the counselee to find out some things on
his own. He goes with him as he does so. As a family counselor he encourages members of the family to discover each
other and get to know one another better. As a group leader
he nudges the group into discussing subjects, feelings, and
ideas that have been tacitly declared off limits. In preaching
he creates two-way communication by anticipating the
questions attentive hearers are prone to ask. All in all, this
approach takes work. Accordingly the minister is a man
who works on the basis of principles rather than according
to rules of thumb.

PRINCIPLES VERSUS RULES

One of the purposes of *rules* is to relieve us of the sweat
that it takes to think through a problem from scratch. Much
behavior needs this automatic "programming" so that the
big issues of life can be dealt with reflectively through the

use of *principles*. The vagueness of a principle is removed by translating it into the right kinds of questions. The questions cannot be answered rabbinically. They must be "found out" by clinical investigation, experimentation, and discovery.

Any given pastoral care situation, therefore, must be investigated — on principle — by asking questions and finding out answers. The pastor is a discoverer, even a "scrounger" for seemingly unrelated data that fits into a larger professional evaluation of a situation. As one who functions this way, the pastor professes to be a *professional*.

"Professional": A Clean Concept?

The word *professional* has a tarnished connotation. That connotation is the implication of commercialism, i.e., that a person pursues his work for the sheer love of filthy lucre or base gain. At the outset, I want to disentangle my discussion of the minister as a professing professional from these connotations of commercialism insofar as possible. At only one point do I want to point to the way in which money *does* play a role in the minister's proper conception of himself as a professional. Harry Stack Sullivan used to say that a professional is a person who *does* what he is being paid to do. The meaning of the statement is that the professional is a person who does not neglect or leave undone what he *is* being paid to do while he does something else. He is a laborer who is genuinely worthy of his hire. He gives his employers their money's worth.

A more basic and useful definition of the minister as a professional stems from my use of the word *professing* with the term. The verb form can be defined as a "continuing, open admission, acknowledgment, and confession of one's calling as a minister." When we measure our timidity, ambivalence, and even efforts at concealment of the fact that we are ministers by this definition, we could stand admonition from the Lord to profess more boldly. We *can* be workmen with nothing to be ashamed of, who know how to use the word of truth to the best advantage (II Tim. 2:15; Phillips translation).

Some trends of thought in the general parish ministry are asking for a more definite consciousness of being a "professional" than we have yet articulated. James Glasse explores this issue thoroughly in his book, *Profession: Minister.* He suggests that the advantages of seeing the ministry as a profession are related to the minister's expertise in the field of knowledge and not merely to his adherence to a given set of ideologies. This conception separates the ministry from a "nine-to-five job" and relates it to the demanding qualities of the other great professions. It provides self-respect for the minister as a "man at work in the world" and not as some sort of recluse. Glasse emphasizes the professional minister as one who has specialized in both information and skills appropriate to his profession. The minister professes to be expert in the Word of God, the administration of the sacraments, and the care of souls. Glasse urges the organization of parish clergymen into a professional society as is characteristic of other professions. He suggests that this society be called the American Academy of Parish Clergy. Here emphasis would be placed upon the improvement of the members' knowledge, skills, and self-understanding.

The Use of Principle as a Talisman of the Professional

Seward Hiltner has set out the dimensions of any profession, all of which can be applied to the ministry. He says that techniques are mere means and not ends in themselves to the true professional, that he acts representatively of all members of his profession, that he provides a service, that he accepts the self-limitations of the extent of his competence, and that he functions according to principles rather than according to rules of thumb.[1] His last point is the one which strikes me to be at the heart of the matter. The minister who functions professionally does so according to basic operating principles and not according to rules of thumb. This approach separates the functioning professional from the hit-or-miss, trial and error, "rule of thumb for everyone" kind of unskilled laborer in the vineyards of the Lord.

BASIC PRINCIPLES OF PASTORAL CARE

Therefore, I should like to describe the most important basic principles for functioning professionally as a minister as I see them. If a minister follows these basic principles he can begin immediately to appraise given pastoral situations — personal or congregational — which he is now facing or is about to face. He can use these principles as questions to ask himself and to answer himself through study and reflection upon the situation facing him, and he can follow these principles in making clinical decisions as to what to do in critical situations.

The Principle of Inspection

The professional minister does not have pat solutions for every problem. Instead he *inspects* each situation carefully. On the basis of his accumulated knowledge, sensitivity, and pastoral evaluation, he searches for an appropriate approach to that particular situation.

Specific data are required for an adequate inspection of a situation. For example, a person's age, sex, marital status, parental responsibilities, occupational demands, the way in which he came to the attention of the pastor, the kinds of commitments he has made to others about the problem he presents, the number and kinds of other persons to whom he has talked about the situation, his relationship to the church for which the pastor is responsible and to the people who are members of that parish — these are a few of the facts needed.

The pastor consciously trains himself to use *all* his senses in observing. The professionally oriented minister is factually concerned. He is data-conscious. He insists upon a fairly complete inspection of the data. He either smokes out or waits out hidden facts in any given pastoral situation before he makes any commitment as to what he is to do. He operates under the limits of time in the gathering of data. Ordinarily these limits of time are not as stringent as we are prone to assume. We can be much less hurried in most situations than we are. Nevertheless, to the limit of the time that a pastor has to inspect a situation, he does so carefully and somewhat dispassionately. Some ministers like to use personal information inventories, paper and pencil problem area tests, and even personality tests. In premarital counseling many use predictive guides and tests of emotional preparedness for marriage. I have never felt at home using these. Rather I prefer to use the time to become trustfully related to the person as an individual. A pastoral inspection can be done in many ways, but the way should be one that is naturally comfortable for the minister himself and one that actually results in really learning the life-situation of the person.

The Principle of Relationship

The meaning of the data is shaped by the kind of relationship a pastor has to the events and person involved. What he would do in relation to a casual friend, a close relative, an avowed enemy, a member of his own parish or a member of another minister's parish, varies as widely as the different kinds of relationships vary. For convenience's sake, I classify all relationships in four fluctuating categories.

First, we have *informal* relationships to persons in the same way that doctors and teachers do. The teacher has parents who stop him in the grocery store and ask why their child is having trouble in a certain course. We as ministers talk over the back fence to our neighbor. We are asked at a social occasion about our work as ministers. The permanent bore in whatever profession, however, is the one who turns an informal occasion into an occasion to preach, teach, counsel, or otherwise "perform."

We also have very *formal* relationships in which persons exert initiative, ask for help, and reach out to us as their pastor for pastoral attention, consideration, and care. They have defined us distinctly in our role as minister and want us to function fully as minister. These formal contacts happen in settings such as the pastor's study, the occasion of a formal pastoral call, in the hospital room. There are varying degrees of initiative in establishing this formal relationship, and the initiative can come from either side in many forms — a postal card, a letter, a telephone call, a "bump into" contact in the supermarket or on the street, a formal pastoral call. The pastor evaluates what his relationship is and what to do to accomplish the most good, do the least harm, and open the way for a continuing relationship.

In the third place, we have *combined* relationships characterized by both formal and informal interactions. We usually shift from one role to the other quite unconsciously and naturally. The professional minister, however, does not leave his role to nature, chance, or just common sense (which is altogether too uncommon). He makes a point of keeping it clear in his own mind at least and interpreting to the parishioner if need be what his relationship is at a given time. He may ask privilege: "May I speak with you as friend to friend quite apart from the fact that I feel keenly the responsibility to be a good pastor to you?" Or to a friend he may say, "I think I need to bring into clear focus now that I am talking with you as your pastor who cares for you and feels a responsibility to God for your well-being as a member of our parish." Or he may have to say, "In addition to being your pastor, we have known each other for a long time as personal friends. One of the great treasures we have is that friendship. Let's not let our official responsibilities loom so large that we lose sight of our friendship." These are somewhat oversimplified examples of the ways in which a pastor can sense and approach the confusion and clarify his relationship.

Without this clarification, a fourth kind of relationship develops. I have chosen to call it a *confused* one. Anxiety elevates, misunderstanding increases. Confused relationships occur when the pastor operates on secondhand information, dashes in without inspection, and begins to function on a "hunch" basis before he has inspected the situation carefully and before he has chosen his own role.

The Principle of Structure and Control

The pastor is different from other helping professionals in several ways. He is constantly on call. He does not have a waiting list. He mingles with people as a "presence" more often than he waits for them to come to an office. He has a many-sided relationship to people. He seldom has just a professional relationship to them. Furthermore, he cannot "dismiss" his counselees the way a doctor dismisses his patients. He continues his relationship to them. This relationship changes form many times over the course of its history, however long or short that history may be. The metamorphosis of these variegated relationships is a part of the conscious knowledge of the pastor.

It is necessary that the pastoral relationship with a parishioner be a controlled relationship. These "controls" are not ways of dominating persons. They may, unless the pastor is candid and open about clarifying his relationship, become tools of "gamesmanship" whereby the pastor manipulates the person in directions unknown or unwanted by the person himself. Apart from such abuse, however, the factors in a controlled relationship are creative instruments in fostering growth.

1. *A clearly defined role.* The first factor in a controlled relationship is that the pastor and parishioner have a mutually agreed upon and clearly defined understanding of the part each is adopting at a given time.

2. *A well-balanced initiative.* The factor of initiative is an invisible but very real line between the pastor and the parishioner. The degree of initiative — whether to write a card, a note, a formal letter; whether to make a telephone call; whether to call and ask the person to come by for an interview; whether to make an announced or unannounced visit to the home; whether to wait until one meets the person by chance — must be decided by the pastor when he is taking the initiative. Getting "offsides" and knowing when the parishioner is offsides is a skill that can be learned and an art that can be developed.

3. *A place of discreet privacy.* The place where the pastor meets a person has a rich symbolism that speaks nonverbally. Visiting the home of the person puts most of the control over the situation in the parishioner's hands. Yet the pastor's going there is the maximum expression of concern on his part. The office of the pastor represents the maximum of formality. The home of the pastor blends the social and the professional dimensions of the relationship.

4. *An appropriate and adequate time for conversation.* Time has its own symbolism. A hospital visit during visiting hours for relatives is likely to be both social and supportive — and equally likely to be interrupted. At the time when doctors visit their patients, a pastoral visit is likely

to be more formal. At the time the patient is ready to go
to sleep before an operation the next day is likely to be one
of worship.

A home visit to a young single girl at her apartment at
7:30 P.M. is open to misinterpretation. A brief stop at her
desk during her coffee break could be an expression of care
for both her and her employer. A counseling session with
her and her fiancé by appointment would be more formal
professionally.

The decision-making of the pastor on these four factors
of control cannot be done by rule of thumb. It must be
done after careful inspection of the situation and an as-
sessment of the atmosphere and purpose of the pastoral
relationship.

The pastor, more than other professional helpers of people, needs to pay special attention to the structure and controls involved in his ministry to people. What does he mean
to them and what do they mean to him? Do they come to
him, taking the initiative? On what basis of information
and background with them can he move toward them?
Where shall he see them? How can a place of discreet privacy without a clandestine secrecy be found? Do they
interpret his intentions toward them in a way that is
mutually understood to be that of pastor *as* pastor, or is it
all mixed up with other connotations?

These controls adequately established tend to make a
secure, clear-cut, and cleanly professional relationship and
not a sloppy, ill-defined, and anxiety-provoking one in
which no one knows what is going on or to what end or
purpose the relationship exists.

The Principle of Emotional Sensitivity

Scripture enjoins us to test the spirits to see whether they
are of God and to have a wholesome skepticism about the

spirits that motivate people. We are to be as wise as serpents and as harmless as doves. Every minister knows that not everyone who seeks or needs his pastoral care is prompted by simon-pure motives. In fact, we ourselves as pastors are not so prompted. We are called to purify our own religion by visiting the widows and orphans in their affliction and by keeping ourselves unspotted from the world. The great contribution of the behavioral sciences to both our faith and practice is the empirical descriptions they have given us of the motivations of men and women. We have elaborate data on depressed, hostile, suspicious, manipulative, withdrawn, dependent, apathetic, and compulsive persons. The pastor learns these characteristics best in a clinical setting where they are written large before his eyes in exceptionally emotionally disturbed persons. His approach to people will differ accordingly in terms of emotional support, good-humored permissiveness, carefully measured emotional distance, firm resistance, patient waiting with the shy and withdrawn, steadfast trust invested in the dependent, steady warmth with the coldly apathetic, and refusal to panic with the compulsive person. His approach to the same person will also vary according to the person's varying circumstances and emotional states. Sensitivity can be learned; it is not just a natural gift. The professionally oriented pastor does not treat all people the same. Rather, he is committed to the varieties of temperament among people. He identifies the variations with skill and cumulative observation.

The Principle of Development and Process

The person who seeks a pastor does not come to the point of distress which calls for help without a personal history. He has gone through a developmental process which arrived at the present difficulty. Therefore, the skilled pastor has

a way of asking. "When and how did this trouble begin?"
In meeting a disturbed couple in a marital conflict he will
ask, "How did you two people meet each other and would
you give me something of a history of your marriage?" The
pastor is particularly concerned with the religious history
and heritage of the person with whom he confers. He must
understand the personal history in the light of common
patterns of human growth. We have a wealth of data from
the field of pastoral psychology and the behavioral sciences
more generally on how the factors governing a present
condition were formed. Mulling over the situation and
doing research between conversations is one way of revealing gaps in the pastor's knowledge of the background and
the processes involved. We have data on the stages of de-
terioration in marriage conflict, the stages in the development of alcoholism, the stages in the process of grief, the
"tunneling" process toward dying, the development of a
courtship into a marriage, and the factors in the decision-
making process. All these are "hard" data providing the pastor with something more than amateur guesswork about what
may be expected in a given situation. The paster is a harbinger of hope, an interpreter of the "shape of things to come."
To fulfill his promise he must know the shape of things
past. If he perceives himself as a professional he increases
his love for people through all manner of knowledge and
inner perception, attending carefully to the principle of
development and process in human suffering.

Each of the kinds of emotional patterns in relationships,
such as persistent hostility or suspiciousness, has a relatively
well-understood pattern of development behind it. These
patterns can be learned. This knowledge moves the pastor
out of the realm of folklore, patent advice, and magical
thinking into the realm of the dependable data of the sciences of man. All these data are given to us in creation.

They are to be received with thanksgiving and prayer; thereby they are consecrated. There is no contradiction between professional wisdom and personal consecration, for both are indispensable in our professional caring. Abundant resources are available to the pastor who cares enough to learn.

The Principle of Distribution of Responsibility

The professionally oriented minister is not a loner. He does not carry the whole burden of responsibility for the care of those to whom he commits himself in service through thick and thin. Nor does he ditch his responsibility by a quick, impulsive referral to another professional person. He may take several days to evaluate a situation to determine the kinds of persons who can be of the most help. All the while he establishes confidence btween himself and the person who is in need. He may stay by the person in a mere "holding operation" until the right kind of additional assistance is available. When he turns to schoolteacher, physician, parent, rehabilitation experts, social workers, family counseling services, or to another of the myriad of resources that are available today in even remote places, he turns not merely as a cooperator but as a collaborator. Harry Stack Sullivan made a wonderful distinction between cooperation and collaboration. Cooperation is mutual assistance between persons who know that they will hang separately if they do not hang together. It is an experiment in survival as separate entities. Collaboration on the other hand is the work of each for the other's good without regard to his own survival.

The competition between professions is based on "therapeutic imperialism" in which one professional poses as having all the answers and simply tolerates others as they can help him. Or it may be a part of a jealous guarding of "the territory" of each lest it be "invaded," as Robert Ardrey suggests in *The Territorial Imperative*. But the ministry is concerned with far more than "ministerial geography," as Seward Hiltner says. We are in a new era and the new dimensions of pastoral care call for more freedom from role preoccupation and more freedom to collaborate with the persons who can bring hope and help to hurting people. As our Lord Jesus Christ said to John, "He that is not against us, is for us" (Mark 9:40). We can have done with our "juniper bush complexes" and return to the threats of our prophetic task with confidence that there are many people who have not bowed the knee to commercial Baals and are genuine professionals in every good sense of the word. Professional respect can be built on collaboration with each other so that every profession may be genuinely edified.

The distribution of responsibility also includes collaboration with persons who are not professionally skilled. Yet they may have deep and abiding supportive relationships with the person needing attention, consideration, and care. The untutored gardener who bathed the dying Ivan Ilyich in Tolstoy's *The Death of Ivan Ilyich* was deeply helpful in his service. Sometimes the humblest and most unskilled person in terms of professional expertise can sustain a person in need in a way that no one else can. As a rural pastor, I learned to rely heavily on the owner of the general store in the community. He had a knowledge and a wisdom about the community that no one else had. He saved me many hours in finding the people who needed me most. He filled many a need that no one else could meet.

In the New Testament the verb *koinōneō* is the word translated in the phrase *"distributing* to the necessity of saints." The principle of distribution is the community in action as a caring community. The task of the Christian pastor is to mobilize these resources and in doing so to make the fellowship of believers into a true community.

The Principle of Durable and Unbroken Relationship

One unique quality of the pastoral ministry is that we maintain our relationships to people throughout the course of the ministry we have in a parish. Even when we move to another parish and deformalize our old relationships, we are remembered by the parishioners as the pastor who went through unique experiences of theirs with them. He was the pastor who performed their wedding ceremony. He was the pastor who was there when a child nearly died of polio. He was the pastor who kept writing to their son in Vietnam. He was the pastor who stood by them when one of the girls had a child out of wedlock. He was the pastor who confirmed or baptized their children into the fellowship of the church. These memories are nonnegotiable and nontransferable. The principle of pastoral care most significantly summed up here is that of *establishing and maintaining a durable relationship*.

The durability of personal relationships in the pastoral ministry has often been undercut by the common assumption that when a minister leaves a parish he should never have anything else to do with the community. The reasoning behind this assumption is that the old pastor will encroach upon the role of his successor. This is a convenient half-truth that keeps many pastoral relationships superficial and perfunctory. The half of the truth in the idea particularly concerns *formal* pastoral contacts after a pastor has left a parish. He can and should redefine and limit his continuing relationships with the people to *informal* ones that sustain friendship and fellowship without at the same time interfering with the orderly processes of the church's function. If he interferes with the management of the church, makes outside manipulative moves to keep the church going as he thinks it should, and uses his personal friendships among the parishioners to do so, then he does confuse the task of his successor. However, there is not a way that he can successfully disavow the nontransferable relationships. He will reside in these people's hearts in a pastoral identity that transcends the institution of the particular church.

Privileged communication. Our consideration of a change of pastors raises the question of how much of the confidential and/or privileged communication people have confided in a pastor should be handed on to the succeeding pastor. The principle of durable relationships points to an answer to this question. The pastor tells the succeeding pastor those things the parishioner *gives him his permission to tell.* Even then, the pastor gives his successor only that information he *needs* to be an effective pastor. More profoundly, however, he does both the succeeding pastor and the parishioner harm when he tells his successor things which he, the successor, has not earned the right in durable relationships to know. When I know a thing about a person and do not know that person at all, I tend to judge the person on the basis of what I know. If I know the person thoroughly and have a durable relationship with that person over a period of time, then I tend to judge what I know by the person himself rather than vice versa. Thus information as such, out of the context of a durable personal and pastoral relationship, can be worse than useless. It can be a stumbling hindrance.

"A time to keep silence, and a time to speak." When it comes to a choice, as William Hulme says in his book, *Dialogue in Despair,* between telling a person something he is not ready to hear or remaining silent, the principle of maintaining a durable relationship takes precedence and you

remain silent. Job was very right when he said to his counselors, "Oh that you would keep silent, and it would be your wisdom!" (Job 13:5).

A prime test of the counselor. The power to wait for the ripening of a relationship is a prime test of a counselor. Especially is this true in relating oneself to shy and withdrawn persons. In one particular instance, I found that a counseling relationship moved through three or four phases before genuine openness could occur. The first was casual personal contact in a social situation in which I felt that the counselee was observing my movements and what I said more closely than other people in the group. Yet she was, as it were, on the outside of the group. In the second phase the person became a student in a class which I taught. During this time her activity was objective, competent, and diligent as a student, and a steadfast personal friendship between professor and student emerged. Then, in the third phase, a particular crisis in her performance as a student arose. This crisis became the occasion for an interview that resulted in a request for personal counseling on a continuing basis. The fourth phase was the actual counseling situation itself, which extended over a period of months.

A crisis in a pastoral counseling relationship may occur in the latter phases of such a relationship as I have described when the formal interviews come to a close and the relationship is gradually transmuted back into a natural, lasting personal friendship. This kind of continuity is no particular private possession of the pastor as a counselor. Physicians who do psychotherapy often maintain lifetime contact with some of their patients. However, it tends to be more *required* by the nature of the pastoral relationship than in other professions. The pastor often knows no other way than impatience to decelerate an intensive pastoral relationship. Impatience often breaks the continuity of the relationship; as a matter of fact, in reality it does not break it as much as it changes the relationship from a positive to a negative one.

Durable relationships: a test of the counselee. Finally, the test of the spirit of a person most indicative of his or her maturity is a willingness and ability to establish and maintain durable relationships. Many persons who seek our assistance as pastors are like Mr. Talkative in John Bunyan's *Pilgrim's Progress:* "They would rather have done with your company than to change their ways." On the other hand, the hit-and-run evangelism characteristic of corruptions of the great awakening spirit of revival in this country used people and had done with them. The institutionalization of the revival movement by many churches has often aided and abetted a shallow, nondurable kind of "contact" versus that lasting kind of belonging persons most deeply need.

Just as the crucial test of a pastor's commitment is his willingness and ability to establish and maintain durable relationships, so the test of a counselee's intentions and seriousness, in turn, is also this same willingness and ability. Fidelity, says Erik Erikson, is the chief virtue learned in adolescence. Staying by a person, regardless of whether we have done some visible thing to which we can point or said some magic word that presumes to turn the trick, is the better part of being a pastor. Steadfastness is the severest test of human reliance on the patience and comfort of the Scriptures. It is the ground of hope for both the pastor and the parishioner.

The Principle of Recording and Evaluation

The professional pastor has the same community status as the nonprofessional pastor. Yet he functions differently. He is separated from the nonprofessional by specific things he does to learn from his experiences. He does not stop with just helping those to whom he has ministered; he learns from each person himself. He does not measure his effectiveness by the reassurances or the rejections of those to whom he has ministered; he evaluates himself over a period of time on the basis of what his records reveal about himself and his growth.

Record-keeping. One of the best ways of learning from one's own experience as a pastor is by making intelligent and easily kept records of pastoral work. The process of writing records and evaluating them tends to produce a reasonable degree of objectivity. The pastor should see these as sources of revelation of God in human suffering and bases for his own continuing theological education. He learns to evaluate himself without too much elation or depression. He looks upon his work soberly and with perspective. One criterion of effective pastoral functioning is that the pastor objectively evaluates his own work. He writes down the particularly difficult situations. In doing so he "debriefs" his own operations. Such debriefing helps develop his own perspective. He learns things about himself that he can learn in no other way.

One of the uncomfortable side effects of clinical pastoral education is that the overuse of the verbatim report tends to botch the pastor's mind with a lasting aversion to any kind of record-keeping. Students say they have had it! A more varied procedure of reporting, a briefer method of describing the student's work, and a wider use of reenactment in role-playing along with audiovisual aids and electronic recording could help offset some of these bad side effects. But more than that, the pastor of a church needs much less time-consuming and cumbersome methods of record-keeping. I should like to suggest a few such methods.

Sample Member Data Sheet

Name .... (   )

                                                                    Maiden name

Date of birth .... Father's name ....

Mother's maiden name .... Name of family physician ....

If married, date of marriage ....

If a parent, names and dates of births of children:

....

....

....

....

Educational experience ....

....

....

....

Military status and experience ....

....

....

Religious experience and brief history of spiritual pilgrimage:

....

....

....

....

....

Pastorally significant events (with dates) which are public knowledge:

1. *Bereavements*
2. *Illnesses*
3. *Accidents*
4. *Divorces or separations*
5. *Desertions*
6. *Imprisonments*
7. *Drug and/or alcohol use*
8. *Achievements, successes, awards*
9. *Attitudes toward the church*
10. *Etc.*

The church membership roll is a cumulative record of the people in the congregation. Preparing a basic information sheet for a folder on each new member would be one way to start. (See the Sample Member Data Sheet on opposite page.)

The brief pastoral notes. The pastor can quickly make brief pastoral notes on a small, pocketsized note pad to be transferred to a different colored sheet for the membership folder. These notes should especially include *promises* the pastor has made to the person. This noting of promises enables him to keep his own conscience in order and to follow through with durable, lasting attentiveness to the person.

The appointment book. A good way to keep an accurate statistical record of one's activities is through the pocketsized appointment book. If kept carefully, such appointment records themselves are notes that pull information from one's memory.

The critical-incident report. On occasions where huge misunderstandings, open conflicts, and extensive anxiety characterize a situation, a pastor does himself a favor and saves time in conversation if he writes down a day-to-day account of the happenings. This drains off his anxiety and quells his need to chatter to every person who comes near him to relieve his anxiety. It also becomes a permanent record of anxiety-laden events which are easily distorted by his feelings.

The pastoral correspondence file. A referral should be followed with a referral letter to the person to whom one sends a parishioner. Often the person receiving the referral will write a brief report to the pastor. Furthermore, correspondence with the counselee-parishioner becomes a firsthand record. Keeping all these written communications in a file is the most satisfying kind of record a pastor can keep.

The answer to the question of how much of this information should be passed on to a pastor who succeeds us is simple: only the *front* data sheet of publicly known information. Thus the pastor succeeding us knows something about the parishioner. The rest of the information is personal to the pastor who received it first. If the parishioner wants the succeeding pastor to know it, then he or she should be encouraged to do the telling. Expressions of confidence in the integrity and competence of one's successor enable the parishioner to make the shift more easily. As a matter of fact, telling things to the new pastor himself *begins* their relationship to him as their pastor.

Recording such as that described here can be done without spending forever at paper work. At the same time it enables the pastor to work responsibly with his people, which is the essence of being a professing professional.

NOTES

1. Seward Hiltner, "Planning as a Profession," *Journal of the American Institute of Planners* 23 (1957): 162-67.

Chapter 4

The Caring Pastor in an Atmosphere of Social Revolution

I have already said plainly that I believe pastoral care as we know it today is being obviously tempted by comfortable salaries and prestige within the establishment to become at ease within Zion. When the pastoral care movement developed in the late thirties, many of the persons now being tempted were the "protest movement" of the churches and theological education. We protested that the mentally ill were neglected in the communication of the gospel. We protested and defended the rights of the mentally ill, the divorcee, the alcoholic, the homosexual, the widow and widower, the estranged child and youth, the criminal, to be treated as more than "second-class citizens." We are all still protesting their treatment. Our protests are seemingly obscured by the more pressing demands of draftees, militant blacks, drug-users, people who are experiencing alienation from society as a whole as a way of life and not just as a temporary phase in growing up into conventional maturity, as Kenneth Keniston says. The purpose of this chapter is to assess the challenge to the caring pastor of the social revolution as he lives and breathes in its atmosphere.

CONTINUITY WITH SOCIAL REVOLUTION

The field of pastoral care, as I have suggested above, has specific lines of continuity with the contemporary mood of social revolution. This continuity may be one reason why the more vocal critics within the ranks of social reformers are often caustic in the criticism of pastoral care; we have so much in common with them. We too have been critical of conventional theological education, and still are. However, it is a waste of time and expensive print to tilt windmills with persons with whom we have such deep comradeship in social change as we have with persons like George Webber, Gordon Cosby, Clarence Jordan, and many others. Much more productive is the clear drawing of lines of our common bonds.

The Ecclesiastically Dispossessed

First, the pastoral care movement has worked with the people who cannot ordinarily pay a preacher, support an elaborate church program, and comfortably warm the pews on Sunday morning alongside persons who can afford large contributions. The activist of today shares this concern for the poor in an affluent society. These people often cannot even afford the kind of respectability it would take to sit in the average lower-class church, much less the middle-class church. The state hospital patient is the most vivid example. I shall always remember preaching to a Southeast Kentucky State Hospital audience on Mothers' Day, 1947. I set forth the ideals that are expected of middle-class mothers, not knowing how I was being heard. A middle-aged woman patient stood up and said, "Preacher, them's fine words, but what if it ain't in ye to do it?" I reversed my field and dealt directly with her question. I accepted her criticism as a good and honest one. I had *not* taken into consideration the kind of demand that I was laying upon her already drained spiritual resources. I had bound heavy burdens, but I took her seriously at her request that I help her bear them. But my point here is that she would not have been at home speaking out and interrupting the sermon in most conventional denominational or interdenominational church services outside a state mental hospital. She was an outsider to practically all structured religious witnessing. She was at home in a worship service in a state hospital.

My further point is that I was working for nothing. It was before the days that salaries were available through state treasuries to meet the religious needs of these persons. There would have been no one there to answer the question at all or even to raise it in the first place if we depended upon the treasuries of either church or state. This same kind of pioneering spirit characterized the East Harlem project leaders and other leaders of inner-city groups like those in Chicago and elsewhere. "There is more that is worthy of mutual exchange than either seems to have realized to date. So far, there has been little such exchange."[1]

Common Temptations

The same temptations, furthermore, which beset the early development of the field of pastoral care also plague the inner-city, antipoverty concern of clergymen. The temptation of an eschatology that insists on everything happening now is an understandable impatience. Nevertheless it is an impatience that removes any kind of orderly process from decision-making in a movement. Impatience may make a prophet out of a person but it will not enable him to remain a prophet. He is forced into manipulation to make his predictions and hopes come true. He is tempted to use means that remove him from those called to be prophets and put him among those called to be clever. Giving in to these temptations will result in what Hiltner calls "the Holy Grail" conception of one's function. Within the theological curriculum, the "inner-city people" will tend to look askance at pastoral care folks in much the same way we have in the past and to some extent still do view hard-working people in the field of religious education. The religious education people looked earlier at missions workers the same way. Each has shared the apocalyptic sense of "the Holy Grail." Thus there is a continuity, and we do not have a clear enough sense of history to find perspective, confess our mutual faults, and be healed.

The Demand for Interprofessional Cooperation

The same interprofessional challenge, furthermore, faces pastors concerned with inner-city, antipoverty, racial revolution problems as faced the pastoral care people. When we work with the mentally ill or the heart patient, we are challenged to relate effectively to the doctor, the nurse, and to a lesser extent the social worker. The social reformer has served the pastoral care movement well by calling our attention to the challenge of social work to the field of pastoral care. We have been overidentified with the medical profession and have had too little collaboration with the social work profession (note the absence of data in the journals of pastoral care on the subject of the interaction of ministers and social workers and on the subject of differences in methodology required in counseling with the poor, the slum-dweller, and the rural tenant farmer, black or white).

It is one thing for the Christian minister to work with the poor. It is another thing for him to act as if he and only he can bring change now. Social workers have been at this

problem for a long time and are still like the nine disciples
at the foot of the Mount of Transfiguration when the three
disciples who had "seen the light" came down to them: the
nine were frustrated, struggling with an epileptic they
could not heal. The multi-problem family does not yield
to treatment as easily as we would think. We cannot be
helpful alone. The Good Samaritan found an innkeeper
and trusted him. The hard-earned gains of the early pioneers in the field of social work are written in the history
of the care of the downtrodden. The minister can study
that history and take lessons from it. For example, one
difficult lesson is that as surely as being a missionary in
a foreign-speaking population calls for learning the language and thought patterns of the people, working with
the poverty-stricken requires learning a language that has
not yet been written. That language is the language of the
illiterate or semiliterate. The values are the values of those
who learn from life itself and not from reading. If a pastor
has the training and experience of a competent social
worker he has the beginnings of wisdom in the language
and values of the poor.

Learning from the social worker, then, is one point at
which both the pastoral care men and the inner-city, antipoverty, racial equality men must meet in facing a common
challenge by the social work profession. However, dialog
will not be easy. Social workers themselves tend to be more
threatened, as far as my own limited contact is concerned,
by ministers than do medical doctors. Some public school
teachers share this sense of threat. A rational ground for
it is the set of taboos in America against the impingement
of the establishments of religion upon the state and its
agencies. A part of the reason also is that the experience of
social workers with the do-good efforts of churchmen without training has been somewhat dismal. But this is not all

of it. A less rational part of the threat the ministry poses to the social worker is that many social workers got their original impulses for their work from religious motivations. Many of them vaguely sense that their work is a recent secularization of what was originally part and parcel of the work of the minister — teaching and social wefare. Within their own profession they still have institutional evidence of the educational and social welfare functions of the churches. Yet these church agencies have often neglected social workers and teachers because of their more empirical and scientific emphasis. In reaction against a sweet piety that may or may not have any real hardheaded common sense, the social workers' rejection is justified and accounts for some of the resistance of social workers to collaboration with ministers. However, as with ministers' resistance to social workers, some of the social workers' resistance is due to plain ignorance of the kind of training a minister often — not always — does have. Neither the minister nor the social worker is above "therapeutic imperialism." Each tends to feel that his own training and credentials-on-the-wall are all-sufficient. This feeling will not be overcome until pastors and social workers are trained together in an interdisciplinary way. This training should be the combined effort of "church and community" teachers and the pastoral care people in the seminaries.

The Curriculum War

This situation points to a fourth continuity pastoral care men have in common with the exponents of the new social revolution: both have a curriculum battle to wage. Little did educators know when segregation moved toward integration and integration efforts led to a new self-consciousness among black people that the very structure of the curriculum itself would be challenged. The competence of the teachers and professors would be called into question. It was inevitable. The extramural education of the theological student is gradually taking precedence over what happens in the classroom. The main difference is that the student learns directly outside the classroom, but often without supervision and often without a sense of history.

One common cause activists in an era of social revolution have with World War II vintage "protesters" in pastoral care is curriculum revamping to correspond to the reality of the learning situation of the student. This is what clinical pastoral education has been up to for a considerable number of years. One of the things I would like to see is the collaboration of draft counselors with persons who are teaching counseling. Another thing I would like to see is the expansion of the clinical method of study rather than the propagandistic method of study applied to the phenomena of the "black presence" on preponderantly white campuses.

For example, the Southern Baptist Theological Seminary was desegregated in 1949 after much effort on the part of both students and faculty and in cooperation with the trustees. However, a quiet application of the clinical method of inquiry into the life-situation of the students who entered in the early 1950s resulted in a set of conclusions that made us aware of deep gulfs between us. The development of clinical approaches within the resources of a black college in the community has resulted in not segregation, but mutual self-respect and free interchange. The teaching of pastoral care for blacks by blacks has taken place without paternalism and with a "two-way street" of learning between blacks and whites. The principle of indigenous leadership can no more be divorced from the teaching of black people than it can from any other enterprise. The principle of indigenous leadership cannot be separated from the problems of the South Vietnamese. Herein is the crux of both social and military problems; no amount of sacrifice or good intentions will take the place of the sense of autonomy, self-respect, and personal identity of both blacks and South Vietnamese. Paternalism will not take the place of their paddling their own canoe with our cheers and financial encouragement.

However, in the 1950s what I have just said would have been heard by integrationists as a Southerner's race prejudice taking a turn toward rationalization. Yet what I have said seems to be implied in the words of one of the main exponents of black power, John Oliver Killens, when he says that black power "does not teach hatred; it teaches love. But it teaches that love, like charity, must begin at home; that it must begin with ourselves, our black beautiful selves."[2] The building of a curriculum on the inner assumptions of black identity should have occurred to us, but for it to have done so would have required that we enter into the life-situation of the student and teach him in terms of himself alone. Similarly, when we teach the poor, uneducated white minister we will necessarily have to enter his frame of reference and not expect him to be and act like us, forever and a day a stranger to himself. The collaboration between activists and experts in pastoral care would call for this kind of dialog about how the curriculum can be revamped to meet the emerging new community that includes the black and the poor white.

Such an attitude calls for more than a curriculum change and a rewriting of the catalog. It calls for a revolution in the attitude of the teacher toward teaching. He must, if he is to teach in such a new curriculum, undergo a basic change in attitude. He must collect data from the student himself as well as from books. Much that must be taught is within the student, who is yet unaware of it. It is not in the library. This reminds us of the approach of Anton Boisen, who resorted to "living human documents" for his data. From a religious point of view, it calls for a kenotic or self-emptying approach to the student on the part of the teacher. It implies listening as well as speaking, asking as well as telling, seeking as well as answering. Hence teaching becomes an event, a pilgrimage in discovery.

CONTRIBUTIONS OF PASTORAL CARE TO THE APPRECIATION OF THE ATMOSPHERE OF REVOLUTION

At the end we want to point to what the field of pastoral care has in the way of hard-earned gains to offer to pastors and others dealing with the conflicts and tensions and unrest of today.

Participant Observation

The first contribution of pastoral care is the idea of *participant observation* over against choosing up sides and becoming a crusader. The zeal for racial integration is now undergoing a confrontation with questions that should have been asked in the first place: "Where is the black man's sense of identity with which he can truly be himself in the sea of white faces into which he is being integrated?" A contribution from the pastoral care movement, it seems to me, is the sense to stay off the bandwagon of this or that cause long enough to see where the thing is going first. But when one does so, he is likely to be thought of as being for the opposition, as being against those he is not for, and as being a temporizer. In any power struggle the analogy of a married couple in a quarrel with each other is apropos. Once a person has "joined up," chosen a side, he loses much of his capacity to affect the whole situation. Yet in white-hot social crises such as a race riot, a poverty protest, an assault of the student population upon the "establishment," any detachment is taken as treason. The pastoral counselor must be stubborn in maintaining his own identity, knowing that this is his chance to make a contribution. He takes a position of being in the problem without becoming a part of anything but its solution.

This stance of participant observation is what the pastoral counselor brings to the adjudication of such intense social distress as is evident in much of the atmosphere of social revolution today. His experience also can be helpful to pastors directly active in bringing about social change.

The Ministry of Reconciliation

The objective of participant observation, however, is not just detachment. Participant observation is the strategy for the data-collection phase of the ministry of reconciliation. It is the phase of listening. As Jeremiah conducted a "listening-in campaign," so does the effective agent of social change. He does not go off half-cocked just because men all around him are losing their heads. He listens, observes, and inspects carefully.

The ministry of reconciliation is based upon the analysis of covenants and the revealing of the hidden purposes that comprise the individual's self-seeking, the need to hold oneself apart from the honest intimacy of self-disclosure, and the manipulation of others just to see them squirm which characterizes much of the interaction ritual of social conflict. The analysis of covenants reveals defective covenants, the absence of covenants, and the breach of well-meant covenants. The face-to-face confrontation of the parties to such covenants or between contending factions is necessary for the clarification of basic issues and the improvement of communication.

But even with the best of communication fundamental disagreements will remain. Since the word *compromise* has become a dirty word in the English language, I have chosen to say that one contribution pastoral care has to make to the present social revolution is that of an empirical method of *reconciliation* based upon confession and the formation of open covenants openly arrived at by contending parties. We use this method all the time in marriage counseling, group therapy, and crisis intervention with whole families and between groups in a community. The ministry of reconciliation seems to me to be the stance most likely to wear longest.

The emphasis upon reconciliation as an objective has been challenged by William Sloane Coffin, chaplain at Yale. He rightly emphasizes that reconciliation cannot happen until a conflict with the status quo has been polarized. However, concentration upon creation of conflict without an inner commitment to reconciliation cannot effectively bring about change that lasts either. The pastor can no more afford to be in the "objective case and the kickative mood" forever than he can afford to be sweetly pious and always smoothing things over at the expense of integrity and progress. If he is really a *caring* pastor he is both concerned enough to demand change and wise enough to work toward reconciliation of the uproar he creates. He has no right to leave his own mess for other healing pastors to clean up. Neither have we any right to be merely healing pastors who fear the use of the scalpel.

Assessment of Motives for Social Change

If one does not believe in original sin, he is likely to develop cynicism as a substitute. The effective relationship of the pastoral care movement with psychiatry makes us likely to take a worm's-eye view of many otherwise lustrous and high-sounding aspirations of ourselves and others. This understanding is a contribution in its own right of pastoral care to the social revolutionary. The expert in pastoral care cares enough to see the darker corners of men's motivation. Yet he does so with a measure of hope.

I want to enumerate a few of the darker motives one sees in much that passes for a social revolutionary spirit: the avoidance of the more onerous duties of the so-called "un-revolutionary" life — it is just more exciting to go on a crusade than it is to study Ayers's *Source Book of Ancient Christianity*. Another frustrated leader in a crowded track of competition — a medical doctor who plans to be a missionary strives for preeminence among a group of theologians. He pulls rank as a doctor; he attempts oratory, he disrupts a class. None of these satisfy his frustrated desire for leadership. Then he becomes an "authority" on speaking in tongues! A consummately bad student becomes an ardent reformer of the curriculum. A man with a long record of not staying in any pastorate seizes the race issue as a "cause" for his having been dismissed. He becomes a racial revolutionary in his own propaganda about himself. A man with a disturbed and unhappy relationship with his son becomes a middle-aged hippie in peace revolts and anti-Vietnam war protests.

One is likely to read my examples as pure cynicism, but they are not quite as jaundiced as all that. This is the kind of information a good historian looks for when he writes about a particular social revolution. My point is simply that if this is the way history is to be read, then we should examine history-making before and not after the fact. The rich contribution of psychiatry and psychoanalysis to the understanding of extremist behavior has often been used to relieve men of the responsibility of acting in the face of injustice. It should rather be used to enable men to purify their motives as they act. The same act can be performed for better reasons with better results.

I am not suggesting the cynical, worm's-eye view of men's good intentions, therefore. Rather I am suggesting that pastoral care has a contribution to make to the social revolution today by insisting that men assess their own motives and distill them through self-discipline at the same time they would change others.

THE CHALLENGE OF PASTORAL CARE
TO A CREATIVE SOCIAL REVOLUTION

Revolution for revolution's sake has foundered on many historical reefs. Such revolutions are often "full circles again," and the last state is worse than the first. Hence, I have chosen to conclude this small book with a challenge to students and teachers, pastors and parishioners, to be a part of a creative revolution. This challenge calls for some revolutionary changes of both pace and direction in the future of pastoral care, pastoral psychology, and the related field of psychology of religion.

A Twentieth-Century Conception of Science

The impact of the natural sciences of physics and biology is just beginning to be felt upon the scientific practice of the pastoral ministry. The impact is changing the nature of the learning process and the way of interpreting causation and responsibility in a strict sense. Linear cause and effect, $A \rightarrow B$, is now being seen more dynamically as a constellation of variables interacting with each other as *both* causes and effects. This new understanding calls for *factor analysis* on the basis of empirical evidence as the beginning of mature moral judgment. It attacks at its foundation the magical conception of power to control all human variables and to blame one person or group of persons — even God — for everything.

Yet we live in a world in which both magical and scientific perspectives exist side by side in the thinking of the same person. The true professional cannot despise or be a slave to either. He must develop the capacity to make an "existential shift" from one to the other and back again. The pastor must, with genuineness and wholeheartedness, for example, be able both to appreciate, i.e., hold as a treasure, the wisdom and power of the symbols of the church and also to enter into a factor analysis of the unreasonable despair of a parishioner who fears to take communion. This cannot be "role-playing pretense." It must be done "with heart and soul."[3]

This recognition of both the symbolic and the literal, the mythological and the mundane, the magical and the scientific heals the chasm between the educated minister and uneducated man. Whatever else we say about the poor, the disinherited, the ghetto black, we must say that they communicate with their viscera and their sweat, with four-letter Anglo-Saxon language, both sacred and profane. They do not communicate in abstractions, Latinisms, and Hellenisms. Their language is often nonverbal and yet it is heard throughout the earth. It is preliterate. It both transcends and underlies written speech. When reduced to writing it is best found in novels, folklore, and poetry, not in books like this one. The pastor who cannot at one and the same time respect both this language and the language of the scientific understanding of life and faith is ill-equipped to minister wholeheartedly and without cynicism to the poor — the peoples of the earth whose well-being is the eye of the storm of the present social revolution. To do so, he needs a twentieth-century grasp of the levels of meaning in the words faith, hope, and love — four- and five-letter words.

A Reevaluation of Pastoral Initiative in the Lower Economic Classes

Up to now pastoral counseling has been primarily a middle-class phenomenon. In the main, it is an upper-middle-class phenomenon. Class characteristics are one of the conditioning influences on pastoral strategy and tactics. For example, the blasé coziness of the middle-class Anglo-Saxon Protestant minister stands in sharp contrast to both the white mountain preacher and the black urban preacher. These people are a refreshing change from the grunting anal retentiveness of the too-careful minister.

In 1951 Milton Lewis Mason studied the social situation in a semirural community on the edge of Appalachia. He discovered that the lower classes — regardless of race — expected the preacher to take the initiative toward them, to visit them, to be aggressive toward them. In one group the custom was that the pastor and his wife ask this, that, or the other family for a night's lodging and meals when visiting. Among middle-class persons this would be an affront; to these poverty-stricken people it was a compliment. As for going to his "study" for an "appointment" with the pastor, these people made fun openly of such an idea. The concept of multiple interviews in a sequence of counseling was unheard of and was something of a mystery.

Yet beneficial results could be gained by visiting with the whole family and — clan style — caring for them with no secrets hid and no holds barred. They had little or nothing to hide from each other and what an analytically oriented pastor might interpret as "unconscious" was really very conscious to them but simply none of his business until they trusted him enough to make it so.

Consequently, the challenge to pastoral care with the in-group-ness of poverty, race, and clan is to throw the mechanics of counseling as it is supposed to be away and keep the heart of it. We need a fresh angle of vision on the art of pastoral calling. We need to take the initiative and go where people are. At the same time we are shucking off superficial preconceptions of what counseling is, we must enable those whom we visit to shuck off their idea of a pastoral visitor as a sort of "heaven-sent truant officer" to admonish them about "laying out" of church. Otherwise, the good news that we have come to see them for their own sakes alone will not get to them.

The current social revolution, then, is challenging the very *method* of pastoral counseling, formally defined. Pastoral passivity — the nondirectiveness of fifteen years ago — is out. A wholesome initiative is in and much in need of being studied with the same empirical skills we have used to evaluate formal counseling. When we do take this challenge seriously, we will be more in touch with the social revolution at its nerve endings, where it hurts. And I am not merely interested in going where the action is but in going where the hurting is. The riot, the frightened mothers looking for their children, the child caught in a school integration crisis, the 23 percent of fatherless homes among the poor as over against the 6 percent among the affluent — this is where the hurt is and only the beginning at that. But I cannot sit serenely in my office and wait for it to come to me. It hurts too bad for that.

The Pastoral Ministry to Structures

Both pastoral care and social revolution exponents inevitably slam into the bureaucracy. Wheel-spinning and pointless effort consume the day in committee upon committee. The temptation to flee may take over. Yet we are challenged to light a candle and not merely curse the darkness of administrative responsibilities. Now is the time to take a new look at recording accounts of administrative conflicts, resistance movements, and plain obstructionism, These "corporate" records can become the stuff of teaching pastoral care from its complex overview of a whole community in action. Data collection is imperative. Pastors specializing in urban centers may or may not be keeping records of their experiences; they may be doing as early pioneers in pastoral care did — expecting us to take their word at face value. I want to see some clinical records of the intricacies of working with power structures, working against them, and working in spite of them. What actually did happen? How can the professional principle of inspection be applied here?

CONCLUSION

The challenge to caring pastors in an atmosphere of social revolution is precisely that which Alan Paton speaks of in *Cry, the Beloved Country* when he says that the counselors have counseled for everything except the brokenness of the tribe. Such is our plight. Is there no balm in Gilead for the open gashes in our society? I think there is.

NOTES

1. Seward Hiltner, *Ferment in the Ministry* (New York: Abingdon, 1969), pp. 194-95.
2. John Oliver Killens, "Symposium on Black Power," *Negro Digest* 16 (November 1966): 36.
3. Jan Ehrenwald, *Psychotherapy: Myth and Method, an Integrative Approach* (New York: Grune and Stratton, 1966), p. 145.

Bibliography

Andrews, K. R. *The Case Method of Teaching Human Relations and Administration*. Boston: Harvard University Press, 1953.

Ardrey, Robert. *The Territorial Imperative*. New York: Dell, Delta Books, 1968.

Bernanos, Georges. *The Diary of a Country Priest*. Translated from the French by Pamela Morris. New York: Macmillan, 1948.

Boisen, Anton T. *Problems in Religion and Life*. Nashville, Tennessee: Abingdon-Cokesbury, 1946.

Browning, Don S. *Atonement and Psychotherapy*. Philadelphia: Westminster, 1966.

Cabot, Richard C., and Dicks, Russell L. *The Art of Ministering to the Sick*. New York: Macmillan, 1938.

Dittes, James E. *The Church in the Way*. New York: Charles Scribner's Sons, 1967.

Erikson, Erik H. *Childhood and Society*. Rev. ed. New York: W. W. Norton, 1964.

————. *Insight and Responsibility*. New York: W. W. Norton, 1964.

Glasse, James D. *Profession: Minister*. New York: Abingdon, 1968.

84

Hiltner, Seward, and Colston, Lowell G. *The Context of Pastoral Counseling.* New York: Abingdon, 1961.

Hovde, Howard. *The Neo-Married.* Valley Forge, Pennsylvania: Judson, 1968.

Hulme, William E. *Dialogue in Despair.* New York: Abingdon, 1968.

Jackson, Joan. In *Quarterly Journal of Studies on Alcoholism* 15 (1954): 562-86.

Jellinek, E. M. *The Disease Concept of Alcoholism.* New Haven, Connecticut: College and University Press, 1960.

Keniston, Kenneth. *The Uncommitted. Alienated Youth in American Society.* New York: Harcourt, Brace and World, 1965.

Krodel, Gottfried G., ed. *Letters,* vol. 1. *Luther's Works,* American Edition, edited by Helmut T. Lehmann, vol. 48. Philadelphia: Fortress Press, 1963.

McNeill, John Thomas. *History of the Care of Souls.* New York: Harper and Brothers, 1951.

Oates, Wayne E. *Anxiety and Christian Experience.* Philadelphia: Westminster, 1955.

————. *The Christian Pastor.* Rev. ed. Philadelphia: Westminster, 1964.

————. *Pastoral Counseling in Social Problems: Extremism, Race, Sex, Divorce.* Philadelphia: Westminster, 1966.

————. *Protestant Pastoral Counseling.* Philadelphia: Westminster, 1962.

————. *Religious Dimensions of Personality.* New York: Association Press, 1957.
millan, 1952.

Sherrill, Lewis J. *The Struggle of the Soul.* New York: Mac-

Theodore G. Tappert, ed. *Luther: Letters of Spiritual Counsel. Library of Christian Classics,* edited by John Baillie, John T. McNeill, and Henry P. van Dusen, vol. 18. Philadelphia: Westminster, 1955.

Tillich, Paul. *Systematic Theology,* vol. 3. New York: Harper and Row, 1967.

Type, 10 on 12 and 9 on 10 Baskerville
Display, Baskerville